Every Product Manager's First 90 Days

A Workbook for New Product Managers

John Franck

For additional resources or to get in touch with John,
visit First90.co

Copyright © 2020 By John Franck

All rights reserved. No portion of this book may be reproduced in any form without permission from the publisher, except as permitted by U.S. copyright law.

ISBN: 9798694538718

To Caleb

For being the one who believed in me and taught me almost everything I know about being a product manager.

"I attribute my success to this:
I never gave or took any excuse."

Florence Nightingale

Contents

Introduction	1
Chapter 1: The Chicken or the Egg?	9
Chapter 2: You Got the Job! Now What?	16
Chapter 3: Your First 90 Days	23
Chapter 4: Know Your Role	30
Chapter 5: Know Your Team	41
Chapter 6: Know Your Stakeholders	63
Chapter 7: Know Your Customer	75
Chapter 8: Know Your Competition	87
Chapter 9: Know Your History	98
Chapter 10: Know Your Product	108
Chapter 11: Know Your Numbers	128
Chapter 12: Know Your Marketing	136
Chapter 13: Know Your Sales	158
Chapter 14: Know Your Future Product	167
Chapter 15: Bringing It All Together	176
Conclusion	186
Acknowledgements	188
Notes	190

INTRODUCTION

In my opinion, being a product manager is the best job in the world. Here's why: if you were to gather fifteen product managers into a room and ask them to describe what they do, you would get fifteen different answers. Each would be telling the truth, based on his or her own experience as a product manager, but their day-to-day work might differ greatly. Every feature, every sprint, and every product is different which means your work is always changing. You will never find yourself bored as a product manager, and you must always keep learning.

As I started to write this book, which is based on my own experiences and successes as a product manager, I suddenly felt very intimidated by the sheer magnitude of skills and abilities that product managers need to have. As I researched, I read through job descriptions, talked to other product managers, looked at industry leaders, and reflected on my own journey. In some areas I found similarities, and in other areas I felt like a baker who was trying to talk shop with an auto mechanic. It was baffling. How could these people, with the same job title as me, have such different jobs? My unearthing of the dissimilarities went on, and I sometimes felt I was leading myself astray. And yet, I continued to follow the path. I found product managers who knew nothing about code and development, and others who were formally programmers. I spoke to very successful product managers who had never used Photoshop, XD, or Figma; and then I interviewed product managers with UI/UX design backgrounds. You get the picture. So the question was: how do I write a book with the potential to help all of these different people? I asked myself that question for months. Then I trained two new product managers, and the answer began unfolding before me.

What I realized was that, in order to write a book that could cover the scope of talents and skills a good product manager needs, I would have to break down exactly what a product manager is (and must be) at their core. To this end, I identified and defined three key areas that have the power to determine a product manager's success or failure:

Quantifiable Skills: These are the skills listed on a resume – Scrum certified, knowledge of HTML, CSS, Javascript, etc., other certifications. The skills required vary depending on the company that is hiring for the position.

Intangible Skills: These are the skills that an employer tries to figure out in an interview:

Are they intellectually curious?

Do they have a strong work ethic?

Do they possess empathy and self-awareness?

How will this person interact with our teams?

How do they deal with conflict?

Can they motivate people?

How do they lead without having power?

Can they manage upward?

And this list goes on.

When I interview a candidate, I generally spend ninety

percent of my time focusing on these types of intangible skills.

Insider Knowledge: This comes *after* someone is hired. It is the knowledge of the company's sales, marketing, product, customers, and more. It's why onboarding is so very important.

I am not knowledgeable enough to write a book on Quantifiable Skills. I'll leave that to people who went to college for more than four years. Intangible Skills are not easily changeable in people, and require much more than a well-written book. I'll leave writing about that to the psychologists and therapists. This leaves Insider Knowledge. Remember I mentioned that I trained two product managers while preparing to write this book? When I hired my current jr product manager, let's call her *Candidate A* I created a long to-do list before her first day. The list involved tasks such as "Getting to Know You" meetings (which I encouraged her to have with various people at the company), digging through analytics, reading books, and calling customers. A month-and-a-half later, *Candidate A* was crushing her job. As for the other product manager that I hired, *Candidate B,* I also gave him a long to-do list as a starting point. Two weeks later, *Candidate B* told me he had finished the list and was ready for his first project. He never succeeded at his job, and we moved on from him after six months. What was the difference between *Candidates A* and *B?* In terms of quantifiable skills, *Candidate B* was a much stronger product manager when dealing with our tech stack. With regard to intangible skills, both candidates were great team fits; both were very personable and demonstrated the ability to lead. The difference was that *Candidate A* put in more work to understand the company, product, team, and customers. Being a product manager is hard work, which is exactly why I wrote this book. Only those who put in this particular type of hard work can expect to succeed.

Over and over again, companies fail themselves and their employees, from the moment a new hire walks through the door. Everyone is excited about the new person, and their manager greets them with a giant pile of work. They need to get that person working as soon as possible. This often means learning as little as is required to start producing. But this "hit the ground running" attitude ultimately sets the new product manager up for failure. They have the right quantifiable skills, and even the right intangible skills, but they don't know how to apply those in the best way.

That knowledge can take six to eighteen months to learn if there is no purposeful plan. Everyone loses when an employee who has been with a company for a year says, "I wish I had known that six months ago."

This book is not going to teach you HOW to be a product manager. Honestly, if you come across a book that promises you that I suggest tossing it into the recycle bin. Being a product manager is complex; it's messy at times; it requires the intangible skills mentioned above and the right personality type. Even though this book won't teach you how to BE a product manager, it WILL show you how to navigate your way as a product manager.

If you are on the outside looking into the world of product management, don't be afraid. Your past work experience has already started to prepare you for product management in ways you haven't realized. There is much to learn, but don't be intimidated.

If you have just accepted your first product management job, congrats! You are in an exciting time. You get the chance to develop the products that hundreds, thousands, or maybe millions of people will use.

If you are a few years into your product management journey, then you already have a good handle on how things are done. You have probably launched some successful and not so successful products. You sometimes wonder if your job and a zookeeper's job are the same. It's possible that you are in what I refer to as the *Danger Zone* of product management. Perhaps you went through all of the steps laid out in this book when you first started the job, and still believe all that you learned back then to be true. But since then, your company has had turnover, and technology has been changing at an unprecedented rate. The data you learned two or three years ago most likely isn't accurate anymore. Becoming complacent is the biggest mistake a product manager can make. Never stop seeking to improve your learning and elevate what you have to offer.

This next paragraph is the most crucial paragraph of the book. You must do exactly what it says, or you might as well throw this book in the recycle bin as well.

Step 1: Go find your favorite pen or pencil.

Step 2: In the box below, draw yourself as a stick figure.

HOLD ON… I know that about eighty percent of you didn't follow those two steps. You just thought to yourself, "This is a silly exercise, and I don't like writing in books. Also, I have no idea where a pen is." This is precisely why you need to do it. Once the ink touches the page the barrier between you and this clean, unmarred book will be broken. From here on out, you won't hesitate to do the exercises I ask of you in this book. So, please, will you just draw the stick figure so we can move on?

Ok! Now go back and draw a party hat on your stick figure. Your stick figure is celebrating because it knows you are going to make the most out of this book!

CHAPTER 1

THE CHICKEN OR THE EGG?

On the left-hand side draw a chicken and on the right-hand side draw an egg.

Go ahead and circle which one you think came first (don't spend too much time thinking about it, we need to move on to other things).

All right, I admit that it was pointless for you to draw a chicken and an egg. In addition, that was the last time I will make you do something that doesn't have a point. I simply wanted you to get accustomed to writing in the book.

If you are self-conscious about your drawing skills, here is the chicken that I drew:

Clearly I didn't go through art school.

I spent the first eight years of my career in a completely different industry. Around year six I knew I needed to transfer out of that industry and into something that was more viable long term. I had experience in project management and had dabbled in tech. Eventually, I stumbled across the job description of a product manager. I had never met a product manager or heard about the role before that. The instant I read the description, I knew it was the job for me. Everything about the job, and the skills required, made perfect sense. I started looking at job postings, but my excitement suddenly went away. Every posting I looked at had the same requirements: at least two years of product management experience, three to five years of product management experience, ten years of product management experience. Every single product manager job required product management experience. It was the classic chicken and the egg conundrum. How do I get product management experience without having been a product manager? I would guess that you experienced something very similar, unless you moved into a product role from within your organization. Thankfully, as the field has developed, a few associate and junior product roles that don't require any product experience have begun to emerge. However, most jobs still require some experience in the product field.

I found myself stuck. I knew most jobs I applied to wouldn't consider me because I lacked the experience listed in the job posting. I needed a way to get experience without taking a product job.

Then I found the golden goose of getting experience:

Startup Weekends and Hackathons! These are short events that are either cheap or free to attend and teams build real products during them. These events are filled with talented developers, but are lacking in product managers. These types of events allowed me to work on multiple products and even win awards for them. Suddenly my resume had what it needed. I was able to show the experience the hiring managers needed to see. If you are reading this book and looking for your first product job, I suggest that you try to find some of these events in your area. Even if you currently have a product job, you can improve yourself by working on something different from your normal workflow.

Below is a generic product manager job description from Workable.[1] Take some time to read through each of the items below. Circle each one that you don't believe yourself to be strong in. Even if you are already in a product job or have just landed one, I suggest you spend some time working through this.

Responsibilities

- Gain a deep understanding of customer experience, identify and fill product gaps and generate new ideas that grow market share, improve customer experience, and drive growth
- Create buy-in for the product vision both internally and with key external partners

- Develop product pricing and positioning strategies
- Translate product strategy into detailed requirements and prototypes
- Scope and prioritize activities based on business and customer impact
- Work closely with engineering teams to deliver with quick time-to-market and optimal resources
- Drive product launches including working with public relations team, executives, and other product management team members
- Evaluate promotional plans to ensure that they are consistent with product-line strategy and that the message is effectively conveyed
- Act as a product evangelist to build awareness and understanding
- Represent the company by visiting customers to solicit feedback on company products and services

Requirements

- Proven work experience in product management or as an associate product manager
- Proven track record of managing all aspects of a successful product throughout its lifecycle
- Proven ability to develop product and marketing strategies, and effectively communicate recommendations to executive management
- Solid technical background with understanding and/or

hands-on experience in software development and web technologies
- Strong problem-solving skills and willingness to roll up one's sleeves to get the job done
- Skilled at working effectively with cross-functional teams in a matrix organization
- Excellent written and verbal communication skills

Now, take some time and come up with a plan for how you will improve yourself in those areas in the next one to two months. It may take longer for you to feel proficient in one or more of these areas, but you need to find a starting point.

Example: "I struggle to create buy-in or convince people of ideas. Action Step: I will buy the book *How to Win Friends and Influence People,* by Dale Carnegie, and read it in the next month.[2] Then, I will document how people respond when I am trying to create buy-in.

Area One Improvement Plan

Area Two Improvement Plan

Area Three Improvement Plan

Area Four Improvement Plan

CHAPTER 2

YOU GOT THE JOB! NOW WHAT?

With a little luck, you are reading this book within a month of starting a product position. Maybe this is your very first product role, or maybe it's your fifth. Whatever your experience level, there is a steep climb ahead of you. Product jobs aren't like other jobs. When a nurse takes a position at a different hospital, it probably doesn't take him or her very long to adapt. This is because ninety percent of the job will stay the same. Only the location and the environment will change (and the environment will only change slightly). However, product jobs are highly relational and require in-depth knowledge of each unique product. You can't just "jump right in" because there are too many variables. You must learn a completely new culture, mindset, and product guidelines—every time.

This book will help you grow your knowledge base about the product and company you currently work for, and give you the tools you will need to do the same at every company you work for in the future. In my first role, it took almost six months before I felt confident enough to make more significant product decisions. I am typically a very confident person and don't often lack decisiveness; and yet, as I started that role, I realized how much information I would need to make smart decisions. If I didn't have the right information, then I would be making gut decisions on product development, which would have been far too risky. By following the steps in this book, you can expect to feel confident enough to make significant product decisions in two to three months.

I remember one of the first projects I worked on. I dug into the data of how customers were interacting with pieces of content. I went down a deep rabbit hole and reappeared a week and a half later with exciting findings. I went to our senior product manager with my results, which I envisioned might drastically change where we were taking the product. He responded with, "Hmm, interesting." Then he went back to what he was doing before I interrupted him. Was he being rude or short with me? Not at all! He had been around long enough to know exactly what we needed to focus on. He was willing to hear my idea and the reasoning behind it, but quickly knew it wouldn't make a significant difference for the company or the product. At that moment, I was fulfilling my job as a product manager, but I wasn't being *effective*. I couldn't yet be an effective product manager because I lacked certain pieces of knowledge that effective product manager's have.

But that wasn't my only blunder. Don't worry, there were more! Several times in my early career I made a different, but very common, mistake: focusing too much on one factor. In my journey to produce the best, most successful product, I put too much attention on an individual stakeholder, a competitor, a number goal, or another metric. When a product manager zooms in on one factor, the result is never good. For me, this meant only focusing on what one stakeholder needed. From the stakeholder's perspective, the request made sense because it would allow their team to do the things they needed to do. However, by narrowing my focus, I lost sight of the bigger picture. I didn't take the time to weigh it against other possible ideas. I didn't consider how it would impact timelines on other items. I didn't consider if it was needed long term or was simply a short term fix. Ultimately all of these distractions led to wasted development time and subpar product changes.

The goal with each of these chapters is to make you realize that all of the factors I listed above have to work together in order to make a great product. An imbalanced product process will always come up short. Too much attention on only one or two factors will lead to wasted time and effort.

The steps in each of these chapters may feel tedious at times. You might assume you know an answer and will be tempted to skip over that section. DON'T DO THAT! Even if a question is the easiest question you have ever had to answer, take the time to fill it out. The constant battle of a good product manager is to resist personal preference and follow what the research and data is telling them. If you commit yourself to answering each question in this book, you will be learning the essentials of a proper decision-making process.

The first exercise of the book is below. The question is similar to a technique used by large tech companies to test a candidate's ability to think quickly about concepts not directly related to their field. Through these questions, the interviewer could discern how the candidate might parse out problems and think them through. Here are a few of them:

How many golf balls could you fit in a school bus?

How much would you charge to wash all the windows in Seattle?

You're the captain of a pirate ship and your crew gets to vote on how the gold is divided up. If fewer than half of the pirates agree with you, you die. How do you recommend apportioning the gold in such a way that you get a good share of the treasure, but still survive?

There are plenty more that you can find from a simple search. There is also the famous "sell me this pen" exercise. All of these examples test how someone processes problems and reveal whether or not they can think outside of the box (that most people are trapped in).

Similar to "sell me this pen," I have a question that every product manager should answer. Try your hand at it in the section below.

Your CEO comes to you and says that you have three business days to acquire ten new users for the product you now manage. You have zero budget to make this happen, and you can't use existing marketing channels. How do you do it?

Did you answer that question easily, or did it take some thinking? There is great value in thinking through things that aren't scalable. We often get trapped by only considering ideas that we can scale. However, when you break a problem down to a small number (ten users), you can get extremely creative with your solution. I ask a variant of this question when I meet with entrepreneurs who want to bring their product to market: "If you just had to sell ten right now, how would you do it?" Now do that before doing anything else. If you can sell ten, you can sell a thousand.

Keep this section blank for now. We will come back at the end of the book and fill it out.

CHAPTER 3

YOUR FIRST 90 DAYS

My first official job was working for a landscape company. My first day on the job I was handed a uniform and a shovel. My task that day: digging sprinkler trenches. If you have never dug a sprinkler trench on a hot Colorado day, consider yourself blessed. I spent the entire day switching back and forth between a pickax and a shovel. By the end of that first day I was ready to quit. Day two was even worse because I was sore. I didn't quit, though. I stayed with that company for years and worked my way up to a point where I didn't have to dig trenches anymore. Why didn't the skinny sixteen-year-old quit? Well, that question was answered roughly six years before the trench-digging job.

My father always wanted his three kids to make the most of

our time during our summer break. He gave us reading lists and other tasks to make sure we kept learning, even though school was not in session. One summer, he asked me if I wanted to make some money. I'm talking about real money, not the usual dollar and change for doing household chores. He offered me twenty dollars. At the age of ten, twenty dollars was A LOT of money. I was already dreaming about the Lego® sets I would buy. The job was to dig out all the rocks in a section of our front yard. I quickly agreed. The next morning I got up early and grabbed a shovel. I started digging up those rocks at a furious rate for approximately fifteen minutes. Then I was tired. Every few days I spent a bit more time on digging up those rocks, but it wasn't fun. In fact, it was extremely unfun. It seemed like the project would never end. Eventually, I just stopped working on it. My father assessed the situation and offered me a way out. He said I could hire him for ten dollars an hour to work on it. I did, and it was basically finished in an hour. I ended up with $10 and slight feeling of failure for not being able to do the whole job myself.

The next summer came around, and there was another part of the yard that needed rocks moved. My father came to me and said that if I moved them he would pay me forty dollars. However, this time it came with a stipulation: I couldn't quit. There was no backing out this time. I shook his hand and we agreed to the terms of the job. Two weeks and a lot of sweat later, I finished.

The day I started the landscaping job, I knew that quitting wasn't an option. I was going to work as hard as I could no matter how hard the work was. Fast forward to the interview for my first product job. I was interviewing against candidates that actually had product experience. On paper, I wasn't the best candidate, but my future boss saw something in me. He saw that I wouldn't quit when things got hard. I wasn't afraid of what I didn't yet know about the job; instead, I was motivated to learn what I didn't know, and master the skills I would need. I spent my first ninety days feeling very grateful for the job, and simultaneously feeling like an imposter. I sat in meetings where I knew I was completely out of my league. However, the thought of quitting was never an option. I drew from my experiences of standing before a large patch of dirt with a shovel....

"What am I doing here?"

"There are people who are better at this."

"What if my work is not quality?"

"I have so much to learn."

"What if I look stupid?"

"What if I can't do this?"

Do you ever find yourself thinking those same thoughts? When you allow yourself to think that way, you are wasting your own time. Never forget that you were picked out of all the other candidates as the best person for the job. Everyone wants you to succeed. Everyone knows you don't know everything. But you aren't going to quit, and you aren't going to fail. You are going to crush this job and be the best product manager your company has ever seen. Your story may not be exactly the same as mine, but somewhere along the line you had opportunities to quit and you didn't.

I am a huge believer in setting goals for myself. I try to set short, medium, and long term goals for different areas of my life. I don't want to be an average product manager in a company; I want to be the best. My personal long term goal is to be the best product manager in the state of Colorado. There will never be a way to quantify that fully, but it drives me to be better. This personal goal is one of the reasons I wrote this book. If you just started your job, your thoughts are probably more around surviving than thriving. You probably just want to get through the day, or the week, without looking foolish. I want you to believe that you will do much more in your job than just survive. Set a personal goal to be the best product manager at your company. If you're having a hard time pinning such a lofty goal in your mind, then do something more tangible. Now, you might think the next exercise is silly (or it might bring back a memory from elementary school). I almost erased it from the book, but since I'm not a quitter, I decided to keep it in.

On the lines below, write the phrase "I will be my company's best product manager." ten times. You know the rules . . . no skipping exercises! I want you going to work each day thinking about how you can be the best.

1.
2.
3.
4.
5.
6.
7.
8.
9.
10.

That is as much of a pep talk as you will get out of me. The truth is, everyone's first ninety days are full of doubt and worry. You have to learn to manage those doubts, focus on the job at hand, and acquire the skills you need as the days go by.

The first ninety days of a new job are some of the most critical. It is one full quarter in the fiscal year of the business. Your first week will be consumed with all the typical HR-related activities, along with getting set up with technology and your accounts. By the end of your first thirty days, you may be starting to function in your hired role, but you will likely still be limited. In months two and three you need to make an impact. You need to have one clear win in those first ninety days. This might mean helping with a version release, pitching a new feature idea, or creating organization and systems where there were none.

What will your "win" be in the next ninety days?

___

The rest of this book will help you achieve that win. I contemplated making this a first thirty days book, and breaking it down into tasks to do each day. The problem with that, however, is that your manager will have plans for you during those first thirty days, and there may or may not be time to do prescribed book exercises each day. Granted, everyone is different and every situation is different. You may get through all of the exercises in this book in your first two weeks. Or, it may take you three months or more to complete everything. Please don't feel pressured to work through the exercises at a certain speed. However, the sooner you work through them, the more quickly you will be able to make better product decisions; but go at your own pace and the pace that feels right for your job.

CHAPTER 4

KNOW YOUR ROLE

Product managers are like ice cream. When you order ice cream the first question is, "What flavor would you like?" People have different preferences for what they think is good when it comes to ice cream. Similarly, product managers come in many different flavors. Your unique flavor can be found in the type of product manager you choose to be. Your work and life experiences shape the way you act and perform in your job. You also have been influenced, for good or for bad, by previous jobs and managers. All of this impacts how you handle product management. It may not be exactly as your team expects, but that doesn't have to be a bad thing. It means that you need to show the areas that you are strong in. Sometimes a person's best qualities don't come out in the interview process. I have hired several people who surprised me a few weeks later with an unexpected skill that brought great value to their work.

There is a popular meme that you might have seen, called, "What people think I do."[4] There are hundreds of variants of it.

As funny as it is to laugh at these, there is an element of truth. In your new job as a product manager, the meme might read:

What the job description said I would do.
What my boss envisions me doing.
What my team expects me to do.
What I think I will be doing.
What I actually do.

Each of these captions is a little bit different. You have

a responsibility in your first ninety days to gain a clear understanding of your role and emanate that to your team.

In this chapter, we are going to focus on the first two captions from "your" meme. What the job description said you would do, and what your boss envisions you doing.

Let's look again at that generic job posting from the first chapter:[5]

Responsibilities

1. Gain a deep understanding of customer experience, identify and fill product gaps and generate new ideas that grow market share, improve customer experience, and drive growth
2. Create buy-in for the product vision both internally and with key external partners
3. Develop product pricing and positioning strategies
4. Translate product strategy into detailed requirements and prototypes
5. Scope and prioritize activities based on business and customer impact
6. Work closely with engineering teams to deliver with quick time-to-market and optimal resources
7. Drive product launches including working with public relations team, executives, and other product

management team members
8. Evaluate promotional plans to ensure that they are consistent with product-line strategy and that the message is effectively conveyed
9. Act as a product evangelist to build awareness and understanding
10. Represent the company by visiting customers to solicit feedback on company products and services

Now, let's split the responsibilities into those that are tangible and those that are more ambiguous:

Tangible

3. Develop product pricing and positioning strategies
4. Translate product strategy into detailed requirements and prototypes
5. Scope and prioritize activities based on business and customer impact
7. Drive product launches including working with public relations team, executives, and other product management team members
10. Represent the company by visiting customers to solicit feedback on company products and services

Ambiguous

1. Gain a deep understanding of customer experience, identify and fill product gaps and generate new ideas that grow market share, improve customer experience, and drive growth
2. Create buy-in for the product vision both internally and with key external partners
6. Work closely with engineering teams to deliver with quick time-to-market and optimal resources
8. Evaluate promotional plans to ensure that they are consistent with product-line strategy and that the message is effectively conveyed
9. Act as a product evangelist to build awareness and understanding

For each ambiguous responsibility listed above, I would write out clarifying questions to go over with my manager.

- What are the levels of growth and market share we are hoping to hit this year?
- In the past, what has buy-in looked like with internal and external partners?
- How would you define quick time-to-market: weeks, months, quarters?
- Can you show me some previous promotional plans that went well?

- How would you describe a product evangelist?

Whenever there are words related to time or growth in a job description, clarification is important. "Quick" might be two weeks for one company and eight months for another. You can't be successful if you don't know what success looks like in the eyes of your new superiors and team.

You know the job you're in now? The one you landed less than ninety days ago? Find the job description for it. That's right, the actual description that first caught your eye when you were job hunting. Got it? Great. Use it to fill in the section below.

As in the prior example, split up the list of responsibilities based on whether they are tangible or more ambiguous.

Tangible

_____

_____

_____

_____

_____

_____

Ambiguous

―――――――――――――――――――
―――――――――――――――――――
―――――――――――――――――――
―――――――――――――――――――
―――――――――――――――――――
―――――――――――――――――――

Look at what you've listed as the ambiguous responsibilities. What questions do you have about these now? List your questions:

―――――――――――――――――――
―――――――――――――――――――
―――――――――――――――――――
―――――――――――――――――――
―――――――――――――――――――
―――――――――――――――――――
―――――――――――――――――――

Now, take the questions you wrote based on your actual job description—and the three questions below—to your next one-on-one with your manager. While preparing for this chapter, I researched questions to ask your boss when you start a job. I found advice such as, "Ask them what their goals are for you in months one, three, and six." While on the surface that seems like a good question, most managers won't be able to answer it. The truth is they hired you because they are overwhelmed. Either someone left the team (and perhaps the job you are in now), or the overall responsibilities expanded to the point that they couldn't keep up. On top of that, they just hired you, which was extremely time consuming. In a perfect world, they would have mapped out your first six months for you, but the truth is they just don't have time to do that. To that end, the next set of questions are designed to help you get to the core of your manager's needs and expectations

What should I consider my top three goals?

How do you define success with this product?

What skill set or experience of yours were they most excited about during the interview process?

By now you should have more clarity on your role and responsibilities. The last exercise in this chapter involves creating a mental model with your role as a product manager. A lot can be said about how a product manager's job is to protect the team, but it is often a term thrown around with no real application. Creating a mental model allows you to visualize what it might look like in your unique situation. Here is what my personal mental model looks like.

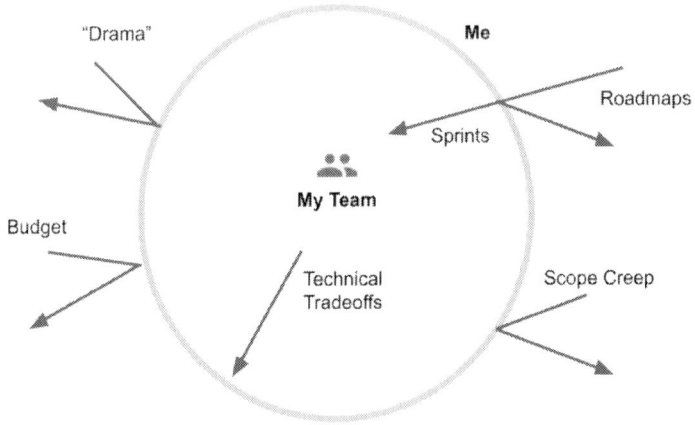

The above diagram shows what I protect my team from, what I let through, and what I expect my team to come to me with. It still over simplifies my role, but it provides a starting point that can be added to. What would your own variation of the mental model look like?

Try creating your own here:

Now that you know more about your own role, it's time to see how you fit within your team.

CHAPTER 5

KNOW YOUR TEAM

When you start a new job, the first few days are a whirlwind of trying to remember names and roles. On one of my first days at a company I once worked for, I went out to lunch with part of my new team. I met twelve people all at once and immediately forgot all of their names and roles. You most likely won't remember what someone does until the third conversation you have with them. Devote yourself to learning the names and roles of the people on your team. Getting to know your team is equally as important as learning your role. As an extrovert, I find joining new teams to be exciting and energizing. If you are more introverted, the thought of getting to know the whole team may be intimidating. I will provide exercises in this chapter, and later chapters, to help this process. My quick advice is to choose someone each day to get to know a little better. It could be as simple as sending a Slack message and saying, "Hey! I'm excited to be here and it was great meeting you the other day. Will you remind me of your role and who you normally work with? I was brought on to work on [insert product name], and I'm trying to learn who does what on the product and how best to collaborate within our team." This will likely lead to an informative conversation, and by the end of the chat you will have a clear picture of this person and their role.

Be Prepared for Drama

Years ago I heard the phrase, "People leave managers, not companies." I believe this is true, but I also think that, "People leave dysfunctional teams, not companies." No position has as much influence on the team culture as a product manager. They work and interact with almost everyone. Ideally, you will step into a fantastic team culture. Occasionally, however, you might find yourself on a problem team. There might be tension, drama, or distrust that has not been, or is not being, resolved. If there are problems within your team, the best thing you can do is work to be a great product manager. You do not need to become involved in drama among your team members. Instead, by doing your job well, you can help to diffuse various issues that may be going on. At one time, I worked with a product manager who always joked that he was like Switzerland: never taking anyone's side, and staying neutral throughout a dilemma.

Here is an example:

Meet James. James has been at Company A for a year and a half as a UX designer. Meet Susan. Susan has been at Company A for six years as a senior developer. James is frustrated because he spends hours figuring out the best layout and design for users, but the developers don't implement them. He studies A/B tests, user interviews, and heat maps to determine the best design choices. Susan has seen the product go through several redesigns in her time with the company. At this point, she is worn down and skeptical of any new design ideas. James sends his designs to the development team, but they are largely ignored. The development team builds what they want to build and only occasionally includes a few portions of a new design. James is frustrated because it seems as if his work doesn't matter. Susan is frustrated because redesigns cause her to backtrack and redo her work.

As the product manager, your job is not to take sides. Your job is to know where this product is going and how each version fits into the bigger picture. You are to work with James and give him the vision for where the product is going. You want to make sure the designs fit into future versions, and that time won't be wasted. Likewise, you work with Susan to explain why design changes will be in the next version release. You emphasize that the future versions will not erase the work that her team is currently doing. You acknowledge each of their views and move the product to a better place. Suddenly James feels heard and validated, and Susan doesn't feel stifled or imposed upon. Each team member feels valued in their work. You did not add to the drama; you resolved it by doing your job. Do your job well, and your team will love you and function better.

Working with Developers

The most precarious relationship that you will have to negotiate as a product manager will be the one you have with your developers or engineers. This relationship exists on a sliding slope and is very easy to strain. The developers or engineers will always have projects that they would prefer to build. They will always have slightly different ideas about the direction a product should take. They are also incredibly smart. When the development team suggests a direction for a product, it is typically well thought out and technically sound. In addition, they probably already have a negative view of product managers; especially if you are replacing someone who wasn't doing a good job. All of this makes for a complicated relationship that you get to manage. I once worked with a product manager who managed to piss off the entire development team in his first two months. The tensions escalated until they no longer wanted to do any work associated with him. In just two months! The interactions you have in your first ninety days will work toward building a foundation of trust and mutual comradery that you will draw from as long as you are in the job. The more exceptional your initial interactions are, the better the implications will be later on. This is even more crucial than the bigger decisions you look forward to making after you get your bearings and pass that six-month mark. The developers may be a tricky bunch, but they can be won over. Building strong relationships early on will pay dividends for years to come. Here are a few guiding principles I try to use when interacting with developers.

- Don't kiss-up to them to get what you want.
- Acknowledge when you don't know something, and ask for help.
- Show that you want them to be happy about what they are working on.
- Try and understand what has happened in the past that was frustrating for them.
- Show that you are willing to change how you operate to make their lives easier.
- Always get them everything they need by the time they need it.

These guidelines have always helped me to maintain a healthy relationship with the development teams I have worked with. Just like in a marriage or a committed relationship, your relationship with your development team will require constant work to make it great. If you are not proactive, it could start to fall apart. I have seen developers who bury their frustration with their product managers. They won't say that things are bothering them, but you can sense it in each interaction. Be proactive in managing those relationships. Being proactive means using emotional intelligence to see how they react to new plans or feature requests. It is being aware of what they find obtrusive to their work. Most importantly, it is protecting them when other team members bombard them with requests and there is scope creep.

What is your development team's biggest frustration right now? Go ask them (they will tell you!), then write it down.

Working with the Rest of the Team

Internal structures can vary from company to company, so don't assume the roles will be the same as in your previous job. If you do, you could end up very confused. In your last job, perhaps you had a dedicated UI/UX designer. In your new role, the designer may report to a different department. You may have to put in a special request every time you need something. This is just one of hundreds of scenarios that you may find yourself in if you are coming from another company or a different type of product job. Your goal, of course, is to get off to a great start with all of your coworkers. An essential piece of this will involve not making any assumptions about anyone. Bring your nonjudgmental A-game to the table in your new role, and let the roles of your coworkers unfold as you learn more about each person. Starting with a clean slate and being open minded to a team that may function differently than your last team will help you assimilate, assume responsibility, and be seen as a team player. To that end, the exercise below is designed to help you quickly learn who does what inside your company. These are the people you will work closely with through the coming months and years. The best product managers are relational, flexible, and don't see people as mere cogs in a wheel. You'll notice that there are non-work related questions for each person. It's important that you know your coworkers for more than just the functions they perform inside the company.

Your company may not have all of these positions, or it might have some not included here. I've also provided blank profile templates at the end of this chapter, to allow you to incorporate a role I didn't cover. Remember, you only get out as much value as you put in. If you have to skip a few until you meet various team members, remember to come back and fill them out later on.

A few general questions that are always advantageous to ask are:

What has your team been working on recently?

What is the biggest challenge facing the team?

Do you have any advice for me?

UI/UX DESIGNER

Name:

- Favorite thing to do after work or restaurant:

- Favorite thing that they have designed?

- How long have they been with the company?

- Who do they report to?

- How will you typically work with them?

- Their personal work goals:

GRAPHIC/PRODUCT DESIGNER

Name: _____

- Favorite thing to do after work or restaurant:

- Favorite thing that they have designed?

- How long have they been with the company?

- Who do they report to?

- How will you typically work with them?

- Their personal work goals:

ENGINEER

Name: _____

- Favorite thing to do after work or restaurant:

- Favorite thing that they have made?

- How long have they been with the company?

- Who do they report to?

- How will you typically work with them?

- Their personal work goals:

ENGINEER

Name: _____

- Favorite thing to do after work or restaurant:

- Favorite thing that they have made?

- How long have they been with the company?

- Who do they report to?

- How will you typically work with them?

- Their personal work goals:

ENGINEER

Name: _____

- Favorite thing to do after work or restaurant:

- Favorite thing that they have made?

- How long have they been with the company?

- Who do they report to?

- How will you typically work with them?

- Their personal work goals:

SYSTEM ANALYST

Name: _____

- Favorite thing to do after work or restaurant:

- How did they become a system analyst?

- How long have they been with the company?

- Who do they report to?

- How will you typically work with them?

- Their personal work goals:

WEB ARCHITECT

Name: _____

- Favorite thing to do after work or restaurant:

- What has been their favorite work project?

- How long have they been with the company?

- Who do they report to?

- How will you typically work with them?

- Their personal work goals:

MARKETING MANAGER

Name: _____

- Favorite thing to do after work or restaurant:

- What drew them to marketing?

- How long have they been with the company?

- Who do they report to?

- How will you typically work with them?

- Their personal work goals:

PRODUCT MARKETER

Name: _____

- Favorite thing to do after work or restaurant:

- What drew them to marketing?

- How long have they been with the company?

- Who do they report to?

- How will you typically work with them?

- Their personal work goals:

Name: _____

- Favorite thing to do after work or restaurant:

- What do they enjoy most about their role?

- How long have they been with the company?

- Who do they report to?

- How will you typically work with them?

- Their personal work goals:

Name: _____

- Favorite thing to do after work or restaurant:

- What do they enjoy most about their role?

- How long have they been with the company?

- Who do they report to?

- How will you typically work with them?

- Their personal work goals:

Name: _____

- Favorite thing to do after work or restaurant:

- What do they enjoy most about their role?

- How long have they been with the company?

- Who do they report to?

- How will you typically work with them?

- Their personal work goals:

So now you have completed profiles for each of the coworkers you will be interacting with regularly. These are the people that you will work with side by side to accomplish the goals of the company. Keep working to develop these relationships. Remember, everyone has goals they are trying to achieve. Some of these goals will align with your goals. Other times, a coworker's goals may seem to flow in the opposite direction of your goals. A good product manager knows how to continually give everyone some of what they want, and gracefully handles the times when everyone can't be pleased. First, produce good relationships; then, produce a great product.

Bonus Tip: Eight months from now when someone does something that helps you out, you will know exactly which restaurant to give them a gift card from, or take them to for lunch.

A *corporate tree hierarchy* is another way to learn, and literally see, how your organization is structured. If you prefer this type of visual, I've provided some blank space on the next page for you to map out the hierarchy of your work environment. I suggest that you write in pencil so that you can edit it in the future when people leave or roles are redefined. You might also consider asking your company if they have an *organizational chart* that depicts your team. If they have one available, it may help you to see where your position fits in, the existing layers of management, how many people have the same role, and your potential career path.

CHAPTER 6

KNOW YOUR STAKEHOLDERS

In product management, the word *stakeholder* gets thrown around quite a bit. To help you understand the term, let's start with a formal definition. The term *stakeholder* first appeared around 1708, and was originally used to describe a person who held bets that had been placed until the bet was won. It still technically retains this meaning, but over time, the way in which this word is used has evolved and changed. Merriam-Webster defines the more contemporary meaning of *stakeholder* as:

- one that has a stake in an enterprise
- one who is involved in or affected by a course of action

When a product manager hears the word *stakeholder,* they generally think of anyone on the C-Level team, and any outside investors. This fits the first definition—*one that has a stake in an enterprise*—quite well. It is accurate to a degree. But what about the second definition, which takes a broader view of who fits into the stakeholder category? This would take you from people within various internal departments, all the way up to (and including) the end user. All of these parties would be considered stakeholders in just one product. Again, this line of thinking is not necessarily inaccurate; however, we don't want to paint a picture that is so broad that we end up saying that everyone is a stakeholder. Every product life cycle, from development through end user, should be honed to include only the most essential stakeholders. This will vary by every product and every feature release; you'll see the groups of stakeholders shift and you'll need to learn how to recognize them. As a product manager who will strive to be the best in your role, you will want to use your knowledge and experience to intuitively know who the stakeholders will be for any given project, and how to consider them as you plan. If you pay attention, over time this skill will become second nature.

But...before any of that can happen, a new product manager must first learn who they are and why their opinion matters.

Non-Stakeholders

We've discussed stakeholders and why they are important. It is equally important to understand who is NOT a stakeholder. There is always someone in the company who thinks they should be a stakeholder on certain decisions. They will seek you out and let you know how and why they should be involved in your project. One of the greatest skills a PM can have is emotional intelligence. While the people that are not stakeholders possibly cannot be told so, they also cannot be blatantly ignored. They probably have legitimate concerns and as they are coworkers, it is only fair of you to hear them out. Then, you need to very diplomatically tell them why the product won't be going in the direction they are suggesting. Treat them with empathy and respect, after all, you both work for the same company. For those times when you will find yourself weeding through stakeholders and non-stakeholders (also known as wannabe stakeholders), here are a few tips that may help you keep the peace:

Only invite true stakeholders to meetings in which the trajectory of the product will be discussed or decided.

Treat everyone kindly and respect their opinions, but also help them understand that not all suggestions can be implemented.

Some people care more about being heard than actually seeing their opinion acted upon.

Be proactive rather than reactive when managing non-stakeholders.

Be empathetic to the coworker who feels like the things they need done are never a priority.

Know your roadmap for the product inside and out, so that you can always justify why the project will progress in a certain order.

"The squeaky wheel gets the grease" cannot be your modus operandi as a Product Manager. You need to have the courage to move a product in the direction you know is best, even if it frustrates a non-stakeholder.

And finally, don't get into the habit of automatically dismissing ideas that certain people bring to you. There is a reason they are at the company. They have skills and value within the company, even if their contributions seem minor from where you sit. It can be refreshing to hear a different perspective, and they may surprise you with some valuable input in the future.

Managing the C-Level Stakeholders

Another key skill that every product manager must have is knowing when and how to push back on stakeholders who are in the C-Level team. Most managers are naturally wired to please their immediate boss, as well as those who run the company, but sometimes a certain directive or agenda from the top can leave you feeling split. There have been numerous times when I faced either doing my job as a product manager or doing exactly what a C-Level executive wanted done. It is not easy to circumvent the priorities of a C-Level executive. This can cause internal tension. Early in my career, I would push through whatever was requested from the C-Level team as my team's highest priority. I felt this was a matter of job security, and the truth is, it was. I still had a job after two rounds of layoffs. I'm sure that wasn't the only reason I was kept on, but I was viewed as someone who would execute the ideas of the top brass. At one company, I waited a full two years before I felt confident enough to push back on a C-Level's plans. Now, I didn't wait that long because they were harsh, arrogant individuals. They still are some of the kinder, gracious people I know. But it took me time to learn how to push back in a way that they would understand and respect. C-Level executives are used to getting their way. When they say, "Jump!" the team says, "How high?" If I chose to tell the executives that their idea had to wait or we weren't going to execute it, I needed to have a good reason. Two years in, I finally felt that I had a firm grasp of the company's history, our tech stack, our most valuable revenue channels, and our marketing verticals. This allowed me to push back in a respectful way when an idea was brought up that didn't align fully with the product direction. Later on in the book, we will talk about the "Squirrel" or "Shiny Object" problem that teams sometimes have. These terms simply refer to anything that diverts attention from the plan. Many CEOs have a "Shiny Object" problem. Part of your job as a product manager is to shield your team from the deluge of "Shiny Object" tasks that might come their way.

Unfortunately, there is no specific formula or a time frame to follow when it comes to pushing back respectfully with C-Level Executives. It is a tricky balancing act to figure out. In my experience, however, most of the CEOs or COOs I have interacted with have been open to and even excited by my alternative point of view. They have understood that they needed my knowledge and expertise, and that of their other product managers, in order to consider the big picture from all angles. Even at the top level, they typically know that a company that only does what the C-Level team wants is a company that is soon to fail.

The exercise below is similar to the one you just finished. I've given you five templates designed to help you zero in on who your stakeholders are. You may be dealing with less than five stakeholders, which is fine. If you feel you are dealing with more than five, only list the five most relevant. Remember, although stakeholders aren't always people inside the building, for this exercise, do include customers as stakeholders. In the next chapter, we will take an in-depth look at customers.

Example Stakeholder
- Name: Jim Wallace
- Position: VP of Sales
- Goals: Increase sales by 3% this quarter by scheduling 5% more product demos
- How do they define a product's success? Jim doesn't care much about the technical details of the product. His team relies on features that are easy to explain and quick for a potential customer to see the bottom-line impact. Success to him is the creation of features that: A) the competition does not have, or, B) perform better. He wants easy talking points for his sales team to draw from when closing a sale.

STAKEHOLDER

Name:_____

Position:_____

Goals

- Goal #1

- Goal #2

- Goal #3

- How do they define a product's success?

STAKEHOLDER

Name:_____

Position:_____

Goals

- Goal #1

- Goal #2

- Goal #3

- How do they define a product's success?

STAKEHOLDER

Name:_____

Position:_____

Goals

- Goal #1

- Goal #2

- Goal #3

- How do they define a product's success?

STAKEHOLDER

Name: _____

Position: _____

Goals

- Goal #1

- Goal #2

- Goal #3

- How do they define a product's success?

STAKEHOLDER

Name:_____

Position:_____

Goals

- Goal #1

- Goal #2

- Goal #3

- How do they define a product's success?

CHAPTER 7

KNOW YOUR CUSTOMER

When you got the interview for this job, what was the first thing you did? You probably started researching to figure out what exactly the company you would be interviewing with does. While doing so, you probably made an assumption on who exactly buys their product. Most people don't stop to question whether their initial assumptions are right. I have been in countless meetings with junior product managers, senior product managers, executives, and CEOs, and watched every one of them make false assumptions about their customers.

Wrong assumptions lead to wrong features being created.
Wrong features lead to wrong products.
Wrong products lead to wrong marketing and sales.

Wrong marketing and sales could be the reason a company isn't around in ten years.

Another mistake is that people assume there is only one type or one persona, when it comes to the end user. Let's say you are tasked with developing an app that will allow people to resell their college textbooks. You go into a meeting, and the entire conversation revolves around college students as users. Sure, this demographic might account for eighty to ninety percent of the user base, but the outliers also need to be considered. What about recently graduated high schoolers who will soon be entering college? What about tutors? What about the parents of college students? What about professors? Do any of these groups make up part of the market that will use this app? Do users behave differently when they are pre-college versus post-college? Do users have different buying behaviors throughout college? It sometimes happens that these outliers lead to the most significant potential for market growth. Therefore, they need to be considered within your product management.

A third mistake can happen when assumptions are made that the most common user is the most profitable user. There is the famous 80/20 rule that speaks to this: 20% of your customers provide 80% of the revenue. At one point I worked on an app that had a high percentage of users between the ages of twenty-five and thirty-five. We assumed that these would be the best users to keep growing on the app. However, as we started to talk to various stakeholders, they pointed out an error in our assumption. We assumed that they needed to connect with a younger audience because their current audience was older and declining. They quickly pointed out that because the platform was highly donation based, the 50+ audience was the most valuable. The 25-35 demographic typically does not donate at the same level or rate as the 50+ demographic. If we had not spoken to the stakeholders, the outcome would have been that the app's growth rate would skyrocket but the revenue would drop.

Take a moment and think about a retail brick-and-mortar store. If you were the owner and founder of the business, you would be able to quickly answer the following questions:

- Who comes in the most?
- Of those who come in, which demographic comes in but doesn't buy anything?
- Which demographic buys the most?
- Are there peak times that people come in and buy more or less?

You would know these answers, because the differences in your consumers and their buying habits would be visible to you. However, when we move things over to the digital world, these differentiations are suddenly not as evident. I would guess that people within your organization are not viewing end users as precisely as they need to. They are subconsciously grouping them in ways they should not be. For example, think for a moment about consumers who leave online reviews. Online reviewers are a small subset of the broader consumer base. Most people who had a decent experience with a product or service won't leave a review. The people who will leave a review, are those who either had an incredible experience or a terrible one. I read reviews on everything I buy. However, I have never personally posted a product review, and I have only posted two Yelp reviews (to get a discount at the restaurant.) For certain businesses, I am in their most valuable market segment. They won't know much about me, or others in my demographic, without putting in a substantial effort. We don't leave reviews, we don't contact customer service, and we don't tag them in our social posts. If the businesses I frequent are only looking at their "visible" customers—customers who leave reviews or mentions on social media—then they most certainly have a skewed view of their customer base.

Recently, I was working with an in-house marketing team on one of our SaaS products. In every meeting, the discussion—from what copy to write, to what ads to create, to which creatives were needed—was centered around the fact that the audience was middle-aged, white males. We were certain this was the customer that would use the product. Every few meetings the Pay Per Click specialist would bring up the fact that inside analytics was showing that close to forty percent of the audience was female and slightly younger. We all ignored this data and kept on with our planning. No one wanted to believe the data because the data didn't tell us what we wanted to hear. Again this all was happening subconsciously. We can become blind to specific facts when they don't align with our world view. As a product manager who is new to the field or to your company, you could also become blind. Maybe you thought you pinpointed your company's customer in the research you did before that first interview, or just after accepting the job. However, six months to a year into the position, your perspective may very well fall in line with everyone else's in the company. This is the problem of groupthink, and every organization is susceptible to it. *Psychology Today* describes groupthink this way, "Groupthink is a phenomenon that occurs when a group of well-intentioned people make irrational or non-optimal decisions spurred by the urge to conform or the discouragement of dissent. This problematic or premature consensus may be fueled by a particular agenda or simply because group members value harmony and coherence above rational thinking."[3] Read that last part again, . . . *simply because group members value harmony* . . . . Doesn't that describe just about every new person in every role new? As a new hire, didn't you want everyone to like you and accept you? Can you see how easy it is to become similarly minded to everyone else in your company?

The next exercise is designed to save you from groupthink. Before groupthink can set in, I want you to dig into and truly know your customers in-depth. You can begin by filling out the customer profiles provided on the following pages. Once you have completed them, answer the follow-up questions. Don't read ahead, simply fill in the questions and then proceed to part two (part one will be skewed if you read ahead). My favorite part about these customer profiles is that long after you are done with this book, you will be able to reference them at a moment's notice. At the end of this book, there is a small section that encourages you to schedule time every six to twelve months to look them over and reorient yourself. When a reminder pops up for you to do this, take a few minutes to skim back through the opening notes that you wrote here. Reviewing this exercise every periodically will keep you heading in the right direction, and help you break free from any false thinking you may have fallen into.

Step 1: Next are five customer profiles. Fill out all five. Even if the product you are identifying customers for seems to only have a couple of distinct users, do your best to come up with five different customer profiles.

Name: _____

Age: _____ **Gender:** _____

Marital Status: _____

Location: _____

Education: _____

Occupation: _____

Annual Income: _____

Goals:

Pain Points:

Motivations:

- Name: _____

- Age: _____ Gender: _____
- Marital Status: _____
- Location: _____
- Education: _____
- Occupation: _____
- Annual Income: _____

Goals:

Pain Points:

Motivations:

Name: _____

Age: _____ **Gender:** _____

Marital Status: _____

Location: _____

Education: _____

Occupation: _____

Annual Income: _____

Goals:

Pain Points:

Motivations:

- Name: _____

- Age: _____ Gender: _____

- Marital Status: _____

- Location: _____

- Education: _____

- Occupation: _____

- Annual Income: _____

Goals:

Pain Points:

Motivations:

👤 Name: _____

🎂 Age: _____ ⚥ Gender: _____

💍 Marital Status: _____

📍 Location: _____

🎓 Education: _____

💼 Occupation: _____

💰 Annual Income: _____

Goals:

Pain Points:

Motivations:

Step 2: Now that you have five customer profiles, go back to each one, and in the upper-left corner, estimate what percentage of usage that customer represents. When you are done, the percentages from all five profiles should equal 100%.

Step 3: Great! Now you can quickly see who uses the product the most. Go back through the profiles again, and in the upper-right corner, write down what percentage of total revenue that demographic brings in. This can be an estimation, but try to have some data to back it up.

Step 4: Find the two profiles with the largest gap between the percentage of usage and the percentage of revenue. One should be positive (higher revenue and lower overall usage), and the other should be the opposite, and therefore negative (higher usage and lower revenue percentage). Now put a negative sign above the higher-usage profile and a positive sign above the higher-revenue profile.

You have now created a quick guide that tells you which user base you should grow, and which one you should not care about. You might be surprised by your findings! If you are surprised, consider all the issues we discussed above. This is the data you will need when you are convincing your stakeholders that you should or should not do something concerning the product.

CHAPTER 8

KNOW YOUR COMPETITION

Apple and Microsoft
Coke and Pepsi
Marvel and DC Comics
UPS and FedEx
Ford and Chevy

Each of these companies—and the rivalry that has gone on between each pair—is well known. These brands are so well known that we don't know one without the other. Each company's biggest competitor is common knowledge, and probably worldwide common knowledge. These companies know who steals part of their market share. They know what their competition is offering and which of their products is positioned as the more desirable choice.

However, if you were to ask the average person to name the top five competitors to any one of these companies, most people would struggle. For example, who is the fifth largest competitor of UPS?

Some companies become laser focused on their top one or two competitors and seem to not care about the rest. They don't care because by the time you get to number three the market share is significantly smaller. However, there is so much for a company to learn from all of its competitors that they are doing themselves a great disservice by ignoring them.

Back in the early 2000s, a particular company was booming while another was just getting started. The booming company owned a considerable percentage of the market, and no one came close to being a major competitor. The smaller upstart went to them and tried to be acquired by them, but the deal fell through. In the eyes of the big company, the newer company was too small, and what they were offering just didn't matter to the larger company. You may have guessed by now what I am referring to. Netflix went to Blockbuster and tried to be acquired by them for fifty million dollars. Blockbuster couldn't see the value in such an acquisition, so they did not push the deal forward. Fast forward to today, and as you probably well know, only one of those companies is still viable. In 2019, Netflix had over twenty-billion dollars in revenue. See what can happen when you don't pay attention to the small competitors? Small competitors can become big competitors. Big competitors can put you out of business.

Over the course of my career, I have spent time working with startups and mentoring at startup weekend events.For me, an instant red flag is when someone tells me about their idea or product and says, "There are no competitors in the market." I immediately think, A) they have been extremely lazy in their research, or B) their idea isn't viable. I have never seen a product or a business that did not have at least one direct or indirect competitor. If you are working on, or thinking of launching, a product that doesn't seem to have competition, I would highly suggest first asking yourself, "Why is no one else doing this?" There have been numerous times when I thought I had an original concept, but after about fifteen minutes of in-depth Google research (this means going beyond the page-one results) or trying to find a domain name, I have quickly realized that ten other people have "already thought of that." This doesn't mean that I had to abandon those ideas; it merely means that I had to refine them, and figure out how to make them unique.

Competition Is Not a Bad Thing

On the flip side of this coin are the people who, when they

discover a strong competitor, immediately get discouraged. Just as forging blindly ahead with a new product (while believing it has no competitors) is very foolish, it is equally as foolish to drop a great idea just because there is an obvious competitor. The assumption is that a competitor is too powerful to be overcome or competed against. Ultimately this comes from a place of either personal doubt or doubt in your product. Here's an industry example I like to use in my coaching: online dating apps. For this example, let's go back in time a few years. Pretend you had an idea for an online dating app when eHarmony or Match.com were primarily the only large dating companies on the market. Most people you shared your idea with would have said to you, "This already exists. eHarmony and Match are already doing it. You won't succeed." This is reasonable logic, but it starts to fall apart when you look in-depth at the market segments those companies were focused on. Between these segments, the market had plenty of room for alternative companies—such as Tinder, Bumble, Hingle, and Coffee Meets Bagel—to have extremely valuable products. The key was to find a slightly different target audience with slightly different needs.

Respecting Your Competition

Have you ever been in the company of a bitter business

owner? Perhaps they are bitter over a new company that is stealing some of their business. Maybe they are angry because an employee left them to go and work for the competition. They treat everyone and everything related to their competition as the enemy. They talk in a negative tone, and throw dirt on every other company—similar to how sports fans talk about their team's greatest rival. Some sports fans would rather talk about how much they dislike their team's rivals more than how their favorite team is doing. They somehow believe that if they bad-mouth the rival team enough, they will feel better about the fact that their team has been under .500 for the past three years. Humans tend to hate things that consistently beat them. There is an interesting switch that happens in sports: fans tend to hate their team's rivals, yet the players tend to have high respect for their opponents. Sure, there are occasions when two players might hate each other, but they are few and far between. There is usually a mutual level of respect between competitors. Despite being on rival teams, they understand the time and dedication it takes to become a professional athlete. Players at an elite level know that the only way they will win is by continually improving themselves.

While writing this book in 2020, Kobe Bryant died in a helicopter crash. I never was a Laker fan or a Kobe fan, but I can respect great players of any sport. Stories started to surface after his death about his work ethic and his "Mamba

Mentality." He would outwork anyone because he wanted to be the greatest. Now imagine if instead of putting extra time in at the gym practicing his shooting, Kobe had spent all of that time stewing over how much he disliked the Celtics. Imagine if he had spent more time criticizing his opponent's play then he did trying to improve his own game. If he had done that, Kobe probably wouldn't have become a household name and the legend that he was.

As a product manager, you could choose to spend your time hating the competition. You could hate them if their product is better in some ways. You could hate them for how much market share they take. However, hating the competition won't help your product. In fact, disliking "the other guy" will have no direct impact on your product at all. If anything, there will be a negative impact because your dislike will occupy precious brainpower. The goal of a great product isn't to beat the competition—it is to give customers the best experience possible.

There was a time when a competitor reached out to me about a potential partnership. At first, I was taken aback. Thoughts ran through my head about how they were secretly trying to gain access to some proprietary knowledge. After I told myself to calm down and decided to assume my competitor's intentions were good, I had a conversation with him. Their product was slightly different than ours.

We only had a small overlap of market share. It turned out that they wanted to go in a direction we did not want to go, and we were going in a direction they did not want to go. It then became apparent that a potential partnership could benefit both of us. I could respect what they were doing, and they could appreciate what we were doing. Were we still competitors at the end of the day? Yes, we were. However, we were competitors that did not have to be enemies.

There are a few other reasons why you should respect your competition: although you may have just started this new job, you never know what the future holds.

What if they acquire your company?
What if your next team member comes from them?
What if you get a job offer from them?

When you treat everyone with respect, you keep the doors open instead of slamming them shut.

The next exercise involves listing the top four competitors to your product right now. You have at least four competitors (whether you think you do or not). If you can't think of four, then hop on Google and do a few quick searches. It should not take you long to find a few more.

COMPETITOR

Company Name: _____

Product Name: _____

- How long has the product existed?

<1 Year   1-2 Years   2-5 Years   5-10 Years   10+ Years

- Growing or Declining? (Circle One)

- How many users? (Estimate)

- Price or Pricing Tiers:

- Top Features:

  #1

  #2

  #3

COMPETITOR

Company Name: _____

Product Name: _____

- How long has the product existed?

  <1 Year   1-2 Years   2-5 Years   5-10 Years   10+ Years

- Growing or Declining? (Circle One)

- How many users? (Estimate)

- Price or Pricing Tiers:

- Top Features:

  #1

  #2

  #3

COMPETITOR

Company Name: _____

Product Name: _____

- How long has the product existed?

  < 1 Year   1-2 Years   2-5 Years   5-10 Years   10+ Years

- Growing or Declining? (Circle One)

- How many users? (Estimate)

- Price or Pricing Tiers:

- Top Features:

  #1

  #2

  #3

COMPETITOR

Company Name: _____

Product Name: _____

- How long has the product existed?

  < 1 Year   1-2 Years   2-5 Years   5-10 Years   10+ Years

- Growing or Declining? (Circle One)

- How many users? (Estimate)

- Price or Pricing Tiers:

- Top Features:

  #1

  #2

  #3

CHAPTER 9

KNOW YOUR HISTORY

"Those who do not remember the past are condemned to repeat it." – **George Santayana**

I love to listen to conversations between people from different generations. Sooner or later they stumble on something that the person from the younger generation has never experienced. "You don't know what a floppy disk is?" "You never used a walkman?" "We used typewriters when I was in college!" and the list goes on. Technological advances have moved so fast in the past forty years that while one generation may have felt completely dependent on a certain device, the very next generation has never heard of it. My wife and I are three years apart in age. Surprisingly, even though three years is not that much of an age difference, we have discovered that we had very different childhoods. These conversations tend to make me feel old, but there is an important piece to pay attention to. Technology moves fast and always has. Think of the technological differences between World War I and World War II. Although only twenty years apart, these wars were strikingly different. Think of how quickly cars became commonplace in the early 1900s. In 1900 there were roughly 8,000 vehicle registrations. Ten years later there were nearly half a million.[4] Think of how quickly home computers became common in the 1980s and into the 1990s. Think of the iPhone, and how only a few years after its introduction none of us could imagine life without a smartphone. What technologies will younger generations be using in twenty years that we, the present generation, will have a hard time comprehending?

"For the young the days go fast and the years go slow; for the old the days go slow and the years go fast." - **Anna Quindlen.**

I remember in the early days of Facebook, they would frequently release major site updates and changes. At that time, people were still getting used to having software updates "just happen" between logins, without the user authorizing them. For most, it was a jarring experience each time. User Acceptance Testing (UAT) wasn't as refined as it is today, and companies were still learning what metrics to watch. It seemed as though whenever Facebook would release an update, everyone would hate it. This happened multiple times: a change would be released, everyone would get upset, and after about two weeks everyone would have adapted. Occasionally you would see a picture of an older version of the app and laugh because it seemed so outdated. This just shows how quickly users can adapt to product changes.

Sometimes users aren't as gracious as the early Facebook users were. They may have hated the redesign, but they still stuck around. You can probably think of multiple products that did a major redesign and then lost a large percentage of their user group. Snapchat did a redesign in 2018 that lost them 3 million monthly users between quarters. If you were one of the product managers on that project, you would have had more than one bad day at the office.

How do you keep from making a "Snapchat-level" mistake? One key aspect is to know the history of your product. Know what worked well, what caused negative user response, and what would cause users to find solutions outside of your product. Now, you may have just started your new product job, so you only have your small sliver of involvement so far. And they may have only briefed you on the most crucial things that happened in the past six months and what is planned for the next one or two quarters. However, to be the best product manager you can be, you need to know what happened in the last two or three years. You must figure out a way to get this information. I have trained several product managers and have been involved in training for other related positions. The same thing happens to almost every new hire: about a month into the job, they come up with an idea (just as I did when I was the newbie), and they get all excited about this idea and run to their boss with it. Their boss then informs them that their "big new idea" was tried a year ago. If that new product manager had done their due diligence and researched the product history, they could have saved themselves the time and effort they put towards pitching an idea that was not new. The more product history you can learn from, the better decisions you will make as a product manager.

I recently read the story of Airwalks in Malcolm Gladwell's, *The Tipping Point 5*. Launched in 1986, Airwalks are a shoe brand that found a niche audience with skateboarders and other "cool" kids in California. They learned how to find and advertise to the trendsetters among teens. A large part of their strategy was to exclusively sell into boutiques and small shops. These shoes were more expensive, but they couldn't be found in the big box stores. If you purchased airwalks in a mainstream store, they weren't the exclusive styles carried by the boutiques. This led to a pattern of trendsetters buying the exclusive Airwalk designs, and everyone else wanting to be like the trendsetters. The kids who looked to the trendsetters "just wanted Airwalks," even if they could only afford the more common versions sold at the big-box stores. This strategy worked incredibly well and grew the company exponentially. Airwalk accomplished having products for two very different users and keeping them both happy. Eventually, however, they stopped selling the limited-edition shoes to the boutiques and small shops. They started to focus only on shoes they could sell everywhere. This was the beginning of the company's decline. Someone in a fancy business suit probably looked at the numbers and asked why they were spending so much to make shoes that barely sold. The numbers on the spreadsheet were accurate, but that wasn't the whole picture. They were only looking at the numbers for the exclusive shoes and couldn't see the correlation between the trendsetters wearing the limited releases and the mass market buying of the big box shoes. The numbers couldn't tell the history that was needed to keep the company growing. Without knowing your product's history, your numbers can flat out lie to you. Later on in this book we will focus on understanding your numbers. A large part of knowing your numbers is never forgetting that they can lie to you.[9]

Digital Life Has Changed Us

I am fortunate to still live in the same city as my parents.

I stop by their house every few weeks. Next year they will have lived in the same house for thirty years. Occasionally we start talking about something and then someone says, "Remember in middle school when . . . " I then open one of the cabinets that sit at either end of my parents' couch and I'm looking at photos from that year in less than 60 seconds. On the contrary, if you asked to see my vacation photos from last year or three years ago, I would have to ask you to wait a little while. My photos are in a giant messy folder somewhere on either an external hard drive or on Google Drive. The images are there, but there is no organization. Part of the difference between my parents' system and mine can simply be blamed on the sheer quantity of photos that can be taken now. I guess that most everyone's photos are in the same digital disarray as mine. We know where our most important documents and folders are, and we backup our systems, but oftentimes our lesser referenced data remains unorganized.

So why mention my parents' picture-perfect photo albums versus my cluttered photos folder? Because disorganization makes discovering the history of anything a challenge. Fifteen, twenty, or twenty-five years ago, if you had asked a business about their events of the previous two to three years, someone would have gone to a filing cabinet and pulled out all of the relevant documents or plans. They likely would have brought forth physical folders and said,

"Here are the drawings of the first version of the product, and here are the boxes of drawings for versions two through forty-two." In today's world, if you ask a team to show you a roadmap of the past year, they will probably struggle to produce it. Teams of today are moving a million miles a minute and documenting only a fraction of their work. Despite this lack of organization and documentation, the information and history do exist. It is not as easy to locate as finding a photo album in your living room or looking in a filing cabinet. It involves going to the right people and asking many questions. It involves digging through (and scrolling through) files to piece together the version history. It involves becoming a part-time detective as you make heads or tales of partial documents or Slack channel conversations.

This next set of exercises will help you dig into the pasts of your company and products. Find the people that have been around the longest and enjoy telling stories. These people know what has really gone on over the years, and they will most likely be glad to share their experiences with you.

How did the company get started?

What was the first real "need" the company or product solved?

At what point did the company grow the most?

At what point did the company experience less growth or decline?

What has been the company's greatest success?

What has been the company's greatest failure?

_____
_____
_____
_____

Product Related Questions

What has been the best release to date?

_____
_____
_____
_____

What has been the worst release to date?

_____
_____
_____
_____

What feature improved retention the most?

_____
_____
_____
_____

What caused the highest amount of churn?

CHAPTER 10

KNOW YOUR PRODUCT

I love the game of football. Football is unique in that physical ability and mental ability have almost equal importance on the field. There are approximately 145 plays that happen in each game. Each play has a defined start and stop. After each play, a team can make adjustments based on the last play. A lesser-skilled team can beat a more highly skilled team by outsmarting them or being more prepared. Being a product manager is similar to calling football plays. You might have the most qualified team, but that doesn't guarantee you will always play the best game. Also, if you execute a terrible play (such as a buggy version release), it doesn't mean you have lost the game. Calling the right play requires knowing what plays have been called before. When you run a football play and get tackled for a ten-yard loss, you don't come back and run that same play again—that would be insane. Instead, you analyze what the defense did on that play and figure out where they might be weaker in the next play. In the last chapter, we looked at ways to find the history of a product. Finding that history is how you learn what plays have been called since the product's inception. Now it's time to learn your product in-depth. This is your football team. You will discover your product's strengths and weaknesses. These discoveries will allow you to move your product further into the areas where it is strong, as well as figure out ways to improve the areas where it is weak.

As a new product manager in a new company, your relationship with the products could take many different forms. You might be taking over for a previous product manager, picking up right where they left off. You might be the first product manager in the company's history. You might be managing multiple products or a single product. You might be developing new products, or moving existing products forward. Every one of these scenarios is typical. By now you should know that this book isn't going to teach you how to operate in every possible situation. Instead, I hope to give you a few questions and exercises to prepare you for any role you may walk into.

In a conversation I had with a colleague not too long ago, I told him that I wished my computer would automatically move my screenshots to the trash after twenty-four hours. I regularly send people screenshots of product layouts, etc., and they often fill up my desktop. He gave me a puzzled look, and said, "Do you not know the keyboard shortcut that only copies the screenshot instead of saving it?" I did not know this shortcut! I was thrilled to learn this "hack," and now I use it all the time. (By the way, on a Mac, it's: Cmd,Control, Shift, 4) Moments like this one demonstrate to me that I don't fully know the tools and equipment I use every day. Life is full of those moments, when one person says to another, "Did you know you could do this?" Suddenly I knew better, but I should have known better all along. I should have dug a little deeper when I realized that my desktop was getting buried in screenshots (a simple Google search might have taught me the hack that is so useful to me now), but I was too focused on other things to do anything about the screenshots. You should never get that complacent with your products. Throughout your first ninety days, and beyond, make it your business to know every functionality of your products—inside and out.

If you have just started a new position, the product you are working on is new to you. You probably looked it up or even tested it during the job interview. You have a general understanding of how it works. I hope that you are reading this book early enough into your job that this next exercise is still possible. I want you to write down in detail your first experience with the product. Ideally this is one or two paragraphs. Don't write this in a business tone or in a way that you would send it to colleagues. Write it down as you would describe the product to a friend for the first time. Write it down as if you are describing your favorite restaurant to a friend. Write down your first impressions of the product, the steps you took to use it, and how long you used it:

_____

_____

_____

_____

_____

_____

_____

_____

_____

_____

Once you have started working on roadmaps and developing features, you will forget your first experience with, and impression of, the product. You will begin to assume that users will know how to use the various product functions because you won't be able to remember not knowing how to use them.

Almost all video games are comprised of a system of levels (either the level of difficulty you are playing against or the level you are on). If you are new to the video game you won't be able to win on the highest difficulty. As time goes on and you "level up" you will be able to win at the harder levels. If you go back and play the easier levels, you will realize how many tricks and skills you have learned as you mastered each level. Now think of your product as if it had levels like a video game. If a new user is a level zero and the highest trained person in the company is a level ten, you are probably currently a level two or three. Soon you will be closer to a level seven on your product. At that point, you will start to think that everyone who uses the product is a seven. But not everyone will reach level seven, and there can be dozens or more reasons why they don't level up as easily or as quickly as you did. This is why you not only need to know everything about your product, but you also need to remember when you were a level zero and understand how users might interact with your product at each level.

What is the first thing a user does when they use your product?

How long before they come back and use it again?

___

What causes the highest number of cancellations or churn?

___

What action do the most loyal users take that other users do not? (e.g., they use it multiple times on the first day, they post three pictures, etc.)

___

For this next exercise, you will need access to analytics. If the product you are developing isn't digital, then you can skip over this exercise. Below is a series of panels that represents the flow a user would take through the product. Figure out what the typical flow is for your product. After that, fill out the second flow. The second flow involves what the *ideal flow* would be for a user—if you could stand over their shoulder and tell them what to do, step by step.

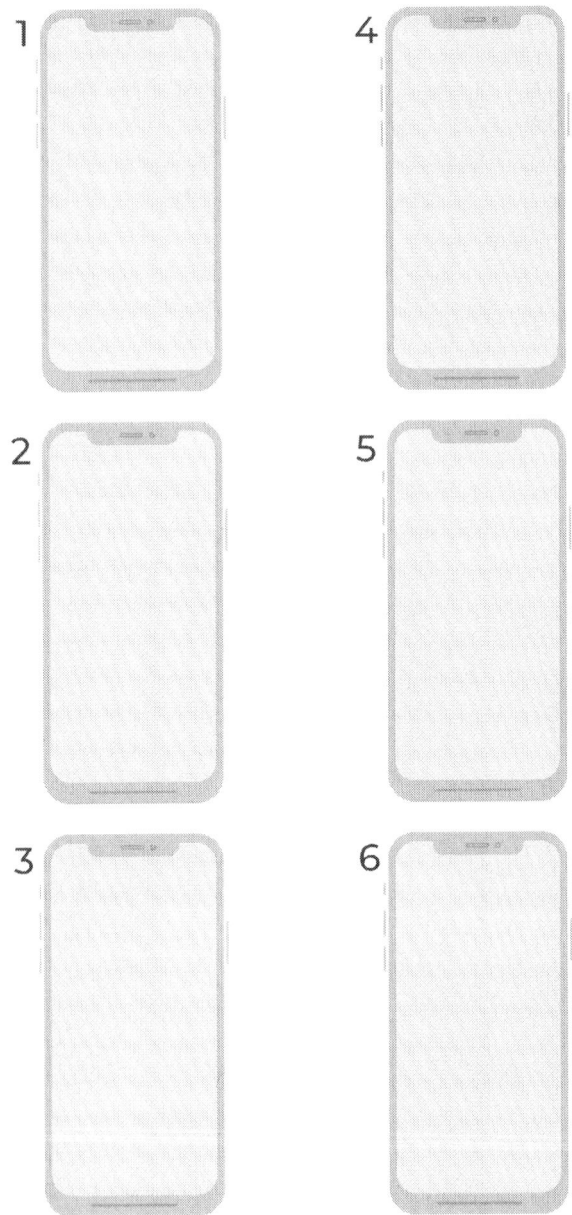

Do the flows look similar? What key differences do you observe?

I once worked on a product that was a job board. People seeking jobs could post their resumes, and employers seeking employees could post available jobs. I took over the product from a previous manager. The site performed decently and made revenue each month. Occasionally the marketing team would promote it or we would A/B test various elements. However, after a while, I started to notice that the job postings were only getting a few applicants. Job seekers were regularly posting their resumes, so why weren't the job postings receiving more applications? In one of our project meetings, I asked this question: "What email does a new user get when they sign up on the site?" The room went quiet. We could practically see the question marks floating in the air before us. No one knew what happened when a new user signed up. I asked a few more questions pertaining to the signup process, and also the process for applying to job postings. The room was still quiet. We had tested changes, improved revenue, and marketed the property, but we had never gone through the site as one of our key user groups. This was ignorance on our part. Maybe your team is more organized, but I'm mentioning this to illustrate that problems can exist right under your nose. Oftentimes you won't hear about your biggest roadblocks and hurdles from your users, and yet a significant avenue for users to be successful with your product may be unavailable to them. If you or your team do not think to test the product from each user group's perspective, you will be doing a disservice to your product. Once we started testing our job board, we found that there was no email provided after a job seeker signed up and no emails to notify them of new jobs. This meant that the employers who were paying us to post a job probably weren't getting as many applicants as they could. Most likely, this also meant that they weren't satisfied with our product. One small product oversight can have a large impact on revenue.

If you have ever been involved with a startup or creating a brand new product, then you know the excitement that comes when you start storyboarding the various screens of the planned user experience. You have a whiteboard, and you sketch shapes that represent screens and little boxes that represent buttons. Then you draw all these crazy lines from element to element, to represent the product's functionality. Eventually, there are so many lines, so many elements, and so many marker colors that only those who witnessed you sketch them can discern what is what. You leave the room knowing that you have mapped out "The Perfect Solution." In the days following the brainstorming meeting, you do everything you can to consider any possible objection to your logic, and to account for any reason why the new product might not perform as it should. You rack your brain and do some research. The idea seems to be bulletproof. Then there is a follow-up meeting. Someone in the room raises their hand and asks a question about how a certain aspect of the product will function. At that moment, you feel like an actor standing on a stage with a trapdoor opened beneath you. You suddenly realize that there are in fact, significant flaws in the design and integrations, things you hadn't considered. Back to the drawing board you go to rework every single element, and try to consider every possible roadblock, once again.

If you are laughing (or even if you are crying) inside right now, it must mean that you have experienced this type of situation. The product you are currently working on (unless it is brand new) has been through this process. There was an original idea, and along the way it morphed into a variant of that original idea. What I love the most about original ideas is that they are full of dreams. They are unadulterated by the inevitable refrains of, "We can't do that." or, "We shouldn't do that." Inside of every original idea are the dreams and the "sky's-the-limit" features just waiting to be discovered—and someone who dared to say, "You know, I had this idea at the very beginning but no one ever pursued it."

Consider the product you are working on right now. What is an idea that someone had for the original product design that never was pushed forward?

_____

_____

_____

There is an incredible book by Kathy Sierra called, *Badass: Making Users Awesome.* I recommend it to every product manager I meet. I highly recommend that you pick up a copy of this book. At the beginning of the book, the author shares two different exercises. The first is answering the question below:

What can someone now do that they couldn't do before your product?

_____

_____

_____

_____

The second exercise has to do with figuring out what broader context your product fits into. The example she gives is for cameras. What is the broader context for cameras? It is a user who wants to make great videos. Inside that context would be several different products such as Final cut pro, the video camera, mics, etc.

If you were the product manager for Yelp, your initial thought for a broader context might be helping users find good restaurants. While this is true, it is too narrowly focused. A better answer would be: Helping users eat delicious food. That is the broader context that products similar to Yelp live in. Many different solutions can come out of that.

What is the broader context that your product fits into?[6]

_____
_____
_____
_____

How Does Your Product Compare?

Remember two chapters ago when we filled out the competitor profiles? Now we are going to fill one out again, but this time for your product. Complete the product profile below just as you did the competitor profiles, but with all pertinent information for your product.

YOUR PRODUCT

Company Name: _____

Product Name: _____

- How long has the product existed?

<1 Year	1-2 Years	2-5 Years	5-10 Years	10+ Years
☐	☐	☐	☐	☐

- Growing or Declining? (Circle One)

- How many users? (Estimate)

- Price or Pricing Tiers:

- Top Features:

  #1 _____

  #2 _____

  #3 _____

Now compare your product to the competition. Where does your product fall in terms of price? How does it compare with the feature list? How does it compare with market share?

Try to plot your product and your competitor's product on the graph. Be truthful. Most companies are not able to dominate on both price and quality.

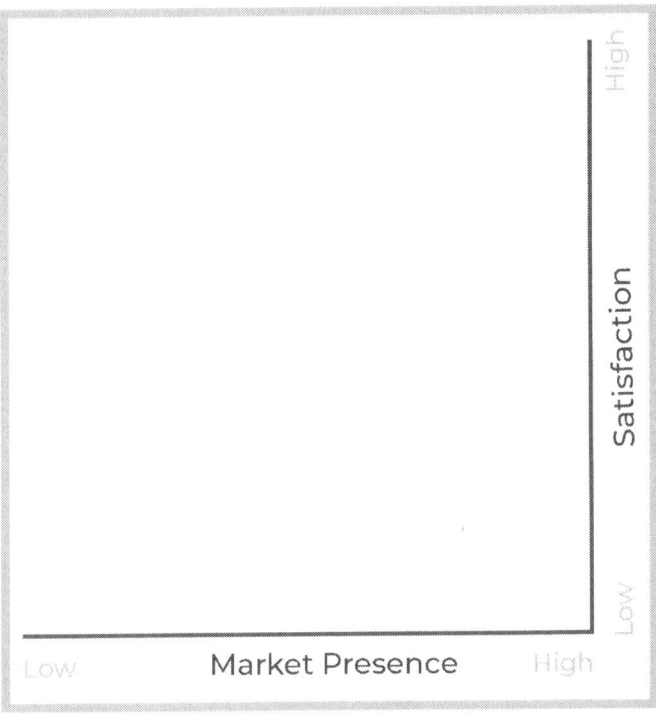

Now plot your product and your competitor's product on this graph. Where does your product fall in relation to market presence and satisfaction? A useful resource when doing this is https://www.g2.com/. This site can help you determine how your company and others have been reviewed. Your company is not a 5-star company. I don't know your company, but I know that every company has its flaws. It is okay to have a 4-star or 3-star review or even a 2-star review. The lower the star rating, the larger the opportunity to improve your product. Remember, you were brought on to improve this product. If it were already perfect, then there would be no need for your job.

Customer Service

Customer service and customer support are among the most overlooked departments in a company. Every time I have to help out with a support issue I am amazed at how patient and kind they are. I could never do their job. Within five minutes of a customer being difficult, I am ready to start calling people names. The reps are unphased. Somewhere along the line, your company may have forgotten that the customer service or support reps are the only real voice that most of your customers ever hear. I once stayed with a terrible web hosting company for years because they had outstanding customer service. By the same token, I have canceled more than a few services because they had terrible customer service. Your customer service or support reps can be the most influential force on how people view your product.

When was the last time you were in a meeting and a customer service rep was invited? Maybe never? I have only rarely experienced this. They may be overlooked but they know your customers better than anyone. Chances are, they know your customers' exact needs and what causes most of their problems pertaining to the product. Too often, executives are happy to sit around and try to guess what the customer wants—but your customer service reps *know* what your customers want. The sad reality is that customer service reps are not empowered to suggest future fixes. They are trained to solve the immediate problem. Your job is to first learn from them and then come up with a plan.

I would suggest first buying them a gift. Maybe a gift card or coffee or whiskey or a trip to the Bahamas? They deal with shitty people every day, and they are rarely recognized for it. Give them a gift and say, "I know I am new here, but I already appreciate everything you do. My goal is to make your life easier. I am going to try to solve some of the issues that you see over and over." Give them a minute to recover from receiving such recognition and then dive into the questions below:

What are the top three questions you get from customers?

_____

_____

_____

_____

How do you answer these questions? How do they respond?

_____

_____

_____

Why do you think our customers cancel/churn?

If you could add one feature, what would it be?

Are there any particular aspects of the product that our customers don't understand?

What aspects of the product do our customers like the most/least?

Have we missed anything important?

Now, take all of this information from customer service and add the ideas to the backlog. I guarantee you will never regret taking the time to connect with this part of your company, and your product will be all the better for it.

CHAPTER 11

KNOW YOUR NUMBERS

Several times a week, as I am scrolling through a feed, I see a certain type of ad. The ad is always the same: a young, attractive person, standing by a Lamborghini (or other luxury car), or lounging in a multimillion-dollar house. The gorgeous young person boasts about how much money they have made in the last thirty days/six months/year, "My business now makes $60K a month, and it's so easy, you can do it too." If you are a product manager, then you are smart enough to figure out that these people are lying through their teeth. People do not make that amount of money just by learning a few "tricks." Even if they did, they wouldn't offer to teach you how to do the same thing for only a small amount of money. If we can move past the absurdity, there is another question to be asked. This question is one

I was trained to ask when I was operating a small business: "What is the profit margin on your income?" Guess what! I can easily start a company that makes $60K in revenue a month, too. My expenses might be $59,999 . . . but I won't tell you that. I will just dangle the promise of big money in front of you until you buy my $49 course. Numbers lie to us every day. Some people make numbers lie on purpose, and sometimes numbers lie to us because we don't take the time to see what is really there.

The first order of business before making any decisions or changes to your product is to make sure your numbers and data are correct. Are the numbers that you are looking at accurate? Once, I worked on a project where we acquired a website. Before purchasing the site, we asked to see their analytics. Based on the analytics, we were generally happy with how the site was performing and how much traffic was coming in. After we acquired it, however, we made a discovery. Over half of the pages didn't have analytics tracking codes on them. Thankfully this was a pleasant surprise because it meant that the traffic was actually double what the partial analytics had indicated. This is an example of how you can be looking at the right numbers but still have the wrong data. I have also experienced every page on a website being counted twice due to an analytics code error. We often think of analytics and data as the one source of truth. However, if your product is regularly pushing out updates and has had "too many cooks in the kitchen," there is a high likelihood that your numbers aren't quite right. It is best to never assume and always double check.

A quote I like is, "What you pay attention to gets improved." Another variant of this is, "What you pay attention to grows." This simple concept could be interpreted to mean, "Whatever numbers you focus on will start to improve." I like that, and it makes me feel warm and fuzzy inside. However, there can be a dark side. For a product I once managed, my team created an automation that would notify us in Slack when a customer's payment failed or their order was canceled. This allowed us to keep a pulse on how the product was doing. Our conversations started revolving around reducing churn. We focused on improving customer experiences and added messaging that discouraged users from canceling. All with the singular focus to reduce churn. *What you pay attention to gets improved.* The problem was that by viewing those numbers throughout the day, it appeared to be a more significant problem than it was. At one point, our marketing manager asked what our churn percentage was. In everyone's minds we had a problem with churn. When we pulled the numbers, our churn rate was below two percent! In comparison, an acceptable churn rate in many industries is five to seven percent. Not only did we not have a problem with churn, but we were doing better than most companies. By having those numbers always in front of us, we turned them into a problem that didn't exist.

What you pay attention to gets improved. This is still a useful concept as long as you are careful with it. On the wall right next to my desk I have a large drawing of a thermometer. It shows the growth number I want one of our products to hit during the year. Every week on Thursday I pull the new numbers and fill in the thermometer. I see that thermometer every time I get up from or come back to my desk. It is the first thing I see when I walk in each morning, and the last thing I see before I leave for the day. Those numbers stare back at me. I am continually thinking about growth and retention. I don't know the percentage, but I know there is a much higher chance I will hit my goal by merely having the numbers where I will see them often.

What is your product's numerical goal for this year?

Here is a tracker for you to measure your goal on. Write your goal and the date you want to hit it at the top. If you can, put this tracker right next to your desk.

You just made your most impactful move towards hitting that goal.

For further reading, check out *The Four Disciplines of Execution,* by Chris McChesney and Sean Covey.[7]

As a product manager, you will ask for important numbers all the time. When you do, you will need to make sure you are asking for (and getting) the correct numbers—follow this up with protecting those numbers, and then taking action on those numbers.

Now it's time to do some data gathering. Some of these will be quick to answer, and others will require outside help.

How many people have used your product in the last year?

How many people have used your product in the last thirty days?

What percentage of people used your product one time and never came back?

[ ]

What percentage of your users are male?
What percentage are female?

[ ]

What age demographic uses your product the most?

[ ]

How many times in a week does the average person use your product?

[ ]

When during the week is your product most heavily used?

[ ]

What is your predicted growth rate for the next year?

[ ]

How many paying customers do you have?

How many users have an account?

CHAPTER 12

KNOW YOUR MARKETING

Every department in a company thinks about marketing.

When you think about marketing and marketers, you probably have one of two reactions: either you think of them as superheroes who can make people convert, get email addresses, and drive sales; or you think of them as snake oil salesmen. Depending on your past interactions, you have either a positive or a negative opinion of marketers. The difference between an honest marketer and a shady one is simple: is it a good product? There is no need for deceitful or unethical marketing methods if a product performs as it should.

I have drifted in and out of the marketing world over the

past ten years. Early on I was involved in SEO. Back then, SEO was like the wild west. You could either rank a website the legitimate way (white hat) or bend the rules and force your ranking (black hat). Early web designers sometimes "cheated the system" with SEO by filling up the edges of their web pages with keywords and then making the font color the same as the background color (white on white). I found this hilarious, and so did many marketers until Google released an update and penalized every site that utilized this shady tactic. From those early SEO days, I learned that the only way to have a sustainable business was to do things the right way, which meant having a site that consistently produced good quality content. There are no shortcuts to long-term success. A great marketing team understands this.

Have you ever landed on a website or landing page and read about an awesome software? You scroll and scroll and read all of the details, and it seems to be the best product ever, right? Every small objection or question you may have had gets answered with each scroll or click. To make it even better, the product is priced so low that you feel you can't pass it up. You enter your credit card information, hit submit, and prepare for world domination. Then things get weird. You log in, but your experience isn't nearly as smooth as the pages you were just on. You go to perform the task you bought the software for and while it technically works, it's not as magical as it promised to be fifteen minutes ago. You don't feel lied to, per se, but you also don't feel like you were told the whole truth. After an hour, you conclude that world domination will not be happening today, and you make a mental note to take the company up on their thirty-day money-back guarantee.

I have a simple formula I try to follow: the longer the landing page, the more likely the product will disappoint. The shorter the landing page, the better the quality of the product. Products that need to be sugarcoated by marketing tactics are products that shouldn't have been built. I am not saying you don't need marketing. You do! And if you haven't brought your marketing team bagels and donuts yet, you should probably stop reading and go do that. Instead of using fancy marketing tricks to make your features seem more impressive, why not actually make impressive features? With a truly great product to promote, your marketing team will have an easy job.

It's important to give the marketing team a seat at the table with your product team. If you don't, the day will come when the marketing team sends out an email blast or posts an ad, and only then will you realize that what they are saying isn't right. A simple miscommunication between the product team and the marketing team can cause your users to start to get that snake oil feeling. You want your users to avoid that feeling at all costs. The messages they receive about your product should be simple, clear, and demonstrate why they legitimately need your product.

The first exercise in this section is an assignment: talk to someone on your marketing team. Not the head of marketing, but rather, someone who has been with the company for a year or less.

Here are a few questions to ask them:

What is the main thing you believe our product does?

_____
_____
_____
_____
_____
_____

How does our product work?

_____
_____
_____
_____
_____
_____

What sets our product apart from other products?

___

What is the best thing about our product?

___

What is the worst thing about our product?

___

Did you get the answers you thought you would get? My guess is that you received a few responses you didn't expect. Your marketing team may have a narrative in their heads that isn't completely accurate. It isn't their fault, they are marketers and not product people. Marketers want people to buy, so their internal dialogue revolves around converting customers more than it revolves around how the product functions. From now on you should do what you can to regularly have meetings with your marketing team. You could host short summary meetings to let them know about new versions coming out. You may want to include some time for them to ask questions about features they don't understand. They may want to tell you about features the market is requesting, or features they feel the product should have to stay competitive. All of these avenues are valuable and should be pursued. Here are a few questions to ask in your next meeting with your marketing team:

Which marketing channel is most effective for this product?

Which marketing campaign had the best success in the past?

Which strategies used to work but no longer do?

Which strategy are you currently most excited about?

Which social channel is most effective?

What is the average ROA (return on ad) spend?

Have you calculated the LTV (LifeTime Value) of a customer? If so, what is it?

By now, you should have a pretty good idea of how your marketing team thinks, a clear picture of your product's marketing history, and an understanding of the marketing strategies they are planning to use. The final section of this exercise takes a look at your marketing team's current processes, and suggests ways for you to fold those into your future procedures.

How does your marketing team currently learn about new features or changes to the product? Map out the process from start to finish.

Do you think that the current process is effective and sustainable? If not, what needs to change?

Does your product team ever get the opportunity to view marketing materials before they go out? If so, how does that happen? I encourage you to subscribe to all marketing emails, push notifications, social pages, and anything else the marketing team publishes. Keeping an open dialogue between product and marketing will only serve to make each team stronger. The product team wants to create the best product, and the marketing team wants to convey the best message—and everyone wants the product to sell. Open communication is what makes good teams great.

Search

Your next step is to know what people are searching for concerning your product.

As I mentioned at the start of this chapter, I've had first-hand experience with SEO. After college I started a side hustle with a friend doing SEO for local businesses. This was back in the glory days of SEO when you could see the results of your efforts within a month or two. At that time, companies fell into two categories: either they were starting to care about SEO and working to optimize their site, or they had no idea what SEO even meant. The latter—those who didn't have a clue about SEO—were easily dominated on Google, while the early SEO adopters raked in the profits. As the years went on, algorithms and strategies changed, and now nearly every company seeks to have their site optimized. At this point, you may be wondering why we are talking about SEO in a product book. Don't worry, there is a tiny bit of method to my madness. When I worked on SEO for my clients back then, I dug into which keywords mattered the most for their businesses.

Every business has obvious keywords. For example, a landscaping company might use the following: "Landscape company Colorado Springs, best landscaper Colorado Springs, Landscaping Colorado Springs." These keywords are obvious, but they don't matter to a product manager. As you get deeper into SEO strategy, your focus should be on something called "long-tail keywords." These are keywords that are more specific, and easier to rank for. An example of long-tail keywords for a landscaping company might be, "Freeze break sprinkler repair in Colorado Springs." You can see that this is a very specific keyword "phrase," and most websites probably haven't optimized a page around this exact keyword phrase.

This is where we make a connection to products. Imagine for a moment, that you have just jotted down all of the main keywords associated with your product on a whiteboard. Now, if I asked you to also write down all the long-tail keywords and terms associated with your product, could you? That's a slightly more difficult task. Do you know what people are typing into Google to find your product? Are they finding you, or your competitor? By studying what people are searching for, you will gain insight into what they truly are looking for in a product.

It's time to do SEO research for your product, and learn exactly what your potential customers want. Ahrefs is one of the best SEO research tools available, but there are others as well. You want a tool that lets you enter a domain and then returns the keywords it ranks for. It will tell you how many times in a month the keyword has been searched for, how difficult it is to rank for, what position the site ranks for with that keyword, and estimation on how much traffic the site is getting from that keyword.

Keyword		Volume	KD	CPC	Traffic	Position	URL
monday	5	94,000	47	0.15	14,583	1	monday.com/
monday.com	8	17,000	40	–	4,763	1	monday.com/
monday project management	8	3,700	28	–	1,300	1	monday.com/
dapulse	6	2,100	19	2.50	1,151	1	monday.com/
monday app	4	3,400	48	...	1,047	1	monday.com/
mondays	6	6,900	17	–	895	1	monday.com/
monday.com pricing	4	4,300	30	–	841	1	1	monday.com/pricing

Here you can see some of the top trafficked keywords for

the site Monday.com.[8] (I love Monday.com, but this is not a promotion) With keyword research, you can see that they rank for the terms most closely related to their brand. You can also see that people are searching for pricing. However, this information isn't actionable. Let's dig deeper into less common keywords.

Keyword	Volume	KD	CPC	Traffic ↓	Position	URL
graphic design project management software	0	50	7	35.00	4.5	4	monday.com/s/designer-management-software
sample agile project plan	0	50	7	8.00	4.9	4 ↓1	monday.com/blog/agile-project-management-scrum/
video production project management software	0	30	1	25.00	3.8	3 ↓2	monday.com/s/video-management-software

Here we start to see other terms that people are searching for. There are people searching for graphic design project management software and video production software. From this short research, a PM for Monday.com could know that they need to expand features to help graphic designers and video producers.

The next step would be to look at competitors. Let's look up Airtable.[9] Airtable is a competitor of Monday.com. If we skip down to the lower volume keywords, here is what we see they rank for:

Keyword	Volume	KD	CPC	Traffic ↓	Position	URL
roadmap template	0	2,100	9	5.00	13	17 ↑2	airtable.com/templates/product-design-and-ux/expHVXu-L59S55Z9fM8/product-roadmap

Maybe this is something that Monday.com should consider. Again, I am not saying that you need to be involved in how the product appears in search. I am saying that you can use search as an insight into precisely what potential customers are looking for.

Here is an exercise you can do for free with no research tool. Go to the main google page and type in your product or company name then type in the letter "A". Look at these results for Uber:

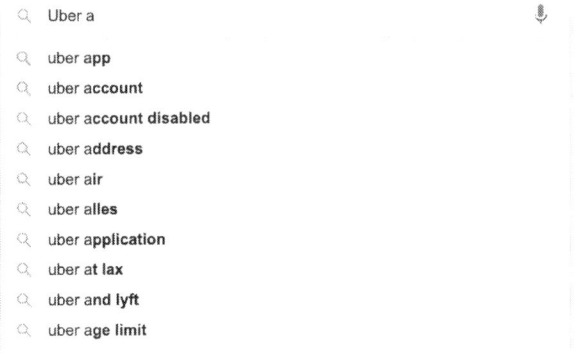

If you were the product manager at Uber, these results would lead you to a lot of questions and probably some tasks.

"Do we have a help page for when someone's account is disabled?"

"How is our application process? Is our page appearing first in search?"

"What info do people need when they land at LAX? Do we have clear instructions about where to meet the Uber at the airport? Do we need to tell them where to meet us in the app as well as with signs in the airport?"

"Should we have a page comparing ourselves to Lyft and why we are the better choice?"

"Do we have clear documentation on the age limit to be an Uber driver? Do we have clear documentation on the minimum allowable age of a passenger riding alone?"

See how much info and research this opens up for your product? Now go on to the letter B:

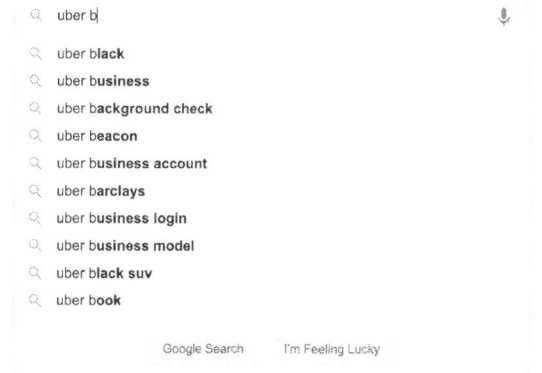

There is space on the next several pages for you to work your way through the alphabet as you research your company name or product. There are checkboxes next to each line. Write out questions or ideas that come up as you study the options that are listed in the search box. Over the next month or so, address or follow up on your findings, and check them off when they are resolved.

A
- [ ] _____
- [ ] _____
- [ ] _____
- [ ] _____
- [ ] _____

B
- [ ] _____
- [ ] _____
- [ ] _____
- [ ] _____
- [ ] _____

C
- [ ] _____
- [ ] _____
- [ ] _____
- [ ] _____

☐

D

☐
☐
☐
☐
☐

E

☐
☐
☐
☐
☐

F

☐
☐
☐
☐
☐

G

☐
☐
☐

H

-
-
-
-
-

I

-
-
-
-
-

J

-
-
-
-
-

K

-
-

L

M

N

O

- [ ]
- [ ]
- [ ]
- [ ]

P

- [ ]
- [ ]
- [ ]
- [ ]
- [ ]

Q

- [ ]
- [ ]
- [ ]
- [ ]
- [ ]

R

- [ ]
- [ ]
- [ ]
- [ ]
- [ ]

S

T

U

V

W

-
-
-
-
-

X

-
-
-
-
-

Y

-
-
-
-
-

Z

-
-
-
-
-

CHAPTER 13

KNOW YOUR SALES

If you went into the last chapter thinking that you didn't like marketers, then you probably don't like salespeople, either. I hope you feel at least a little closer to your marketing team by now. For your next assignment, I'm going to try to help you learn to care about your sales team. They have one of the toughest jobs in the business, with the least amount of security. As I mentioned at the beginning of this book, it is impossible to write a book that applies to all companies and all scenarios. I am trying to hit on the broad themes that can apply to all product managers. If you manage a product that doesn't require a sales team, then skip to the next chapter.

In the last section, we discussed how the marketing team may have a distorted view of your product. Similarly, the sales team may have somewhat of a distorted view. Depending on how their compensation structure is organized, they may be highly motivated to get initial sales but not concerned with or focused on customer retention. You need to know how their compensation is structured, and also be aware of what they promise clients or customers about the product.

It's time for a role-playing exercise. (I know that at this moment half of you just tossed the book in the garbage can. You're thinking, "Role-playing exercise? Are we in high school? I'm a professional!" I get it. I hate role-playing exercises. I don't even like to play charades. The mere mention of group games makes me want to leave the room. However, I promise this one won't be too terrible; it might even be kind of fun. There was this scene in *The Office* in which Michael Scott pulled Jim and Dwight into the conference room.[10] He then made Jim pretend to be a potential customer with Dwight as the salesman. Dwight then had to deal with all the obscure things Jim threw at him while simultaneously trying to sell him paper:

Michael: Boom! Yes. Now, Jim is going to be the client. **Dwight**, you're going to have to sell to him without being aggressive, hostile or difficult. Let's go.
Dwight: All right, fine. [picks up phone] Brrring.
Jim: [picks up phone] Hello?

Dwight: Hello, this is Dwight Schrute from the Dunder Mifflin Paper Company.

Jim: Wow, that's great, because I need paper.

Dwight: Excellent, then you are in luck, because we are having a limited-time offer only on everything.

Jim: Wow, this is my lucky day.

Michael: [whispers] Ask him his name.

Dwight: What is your name, sir?

Jim: I am Bill Buttlicker.

Dwight: Really, that's your real name?

Jim: How dare you? My family built this country, by the way.

Michael: Be respectful, Dwight.

Dwight: Yes, Michael.

Jim: Would you hold on one second? That's my other line.

Dwight: What? No, but I...

Jim: Hello? [laughs] No, I'm just on the phone with this stupid salesman. He's so dumb. Probably just gonna keep him on the line forever and not buy anything. Yeah, OK. [punches button on phone]

Michael: It's up to you to change his mind.[11]

And it goes on.

This next exercise is similar to Dwight and Jim's charade, but not as ridiculous.

Ask your sales team if one of them has a few minutes to do

a sales exercise with you. If the sales team typically conducts phone sales, have them call you just as if you were a potential customer. If they do online demos of the product, have them take you through an online demo. If they make in-person sales calls, go out to lunch and have them pitch the product to you. You get the idea. Get their sales pitch, experience it as if you were a potential customer, then follow up by asking them the questions below:

What are the top three questions you get from potential customers?

___

How do you answer these questions? How do they respond?

What is the most significant barrier keeping people from buying the product?

Are there any specific selling points that work particularly well? If so, which ones?

Have we missed anything important? Got something to add?

Fill in the next set of questions after you have finished talking with them:

What was the first feature they mentioned to you or showed you?

_____

What features were they most excited about?

_____

What intrinsic value did they describe the product bringing to someone?

_____

On a scale of one to ten—with ten being entirely truthful and one being not very accurate—how would you rate them on describing the product? (This isn't meant as a way to shame them but rather to learn how they communicate.)

When they discussed the cost of the product, did they seem apologetic for the price, or did they come across as if the price point is a great value?

Hopefully this exercise went smoothly for you, and maybe you even got a free lunch out of it. To be honest, product managers rarely get taken to lunch, and probably never by a member of the sales team. This exercise was meant to help you become more acquainted with members of your sales team, give you a better understanding of how they tick, and to open a dialogue between you and them to ensure they have everything they need to successfully sell your product. The next set of questions can be asked of anyone on the sales team, your choice.

Who is the most valuable customer?

What's the difference between your most valuable customer and our average customers?

What type of customer is the easiest to get?

What type of customer is the hardest to get?

_____

_____

_____

What is the average lifespan of a customer? (Remember: this is their interpretation and not based on the data we looked at in previous chapters. You want to understand things from your sales team's perspective.)

_____

_____

_____

_____

Are the ideas flowing now for potential features or product improvements? I hope they are! Guess what. It's time to go back and look at the first chapter of this book. Your very first exercise was to answer a question about how you would acquire ten new users/clients for your product. Compare your answer to your sales team's approach, now that you understand it. Maybe you will see your initial idea as foolish and naive, maybe it will seem potentially feasible, or perhaps it is dead on. If it is one of the latter two, it might be time for you to buy a salesperson lunch and make their day! Go back to that early chapter and fill out the exercise that we left blank. Write out how you would get ten new customers now that you have the knowledge from all the other chapters.

CHAPTER 14

KNOW YOUR FUTURE PRODUCT

When I was a kid, we spent a lot of summer days at garage sales. I grew up in a time before Craigslist or Facebook Marketplace, when garage sales were goldmines. If I wander through a garage sale now, as an adult, they just seem to be filled with stained furniture, broken decor, and outdated home technology. My childhood memories of going to garage sales are filled with the feeling of endless possibility and near certainty of finding a real treasure. On one such summer day, my parents brought us all to a garage sale and I spotted this giant box. Inside the box was what we referred to as life-sized "K'nex." Imagine PVC-like pipes of various lengths up to five feet, connectors that allowed the pipes to be put together at different angles, and connectable wheels. Of course my siblings and I had to have this treasure. We snagged this huge box for around ten dollars. For the rest of the summer and for many summers to come, my sisters and I built everything from small buildings, to functional vehicles, to weird art pieces. That box held within it the same endless possibility as the garage sales themselves. And once it was in our possession, it gave me the feeling that, "I can now build whatever I want."

Fast forward ten or so years. I was just starting to get into web design. I was working in Wordpress with zero knowledge of PHP, CSS, or HTML. In reality, I probably had no business trying to be a web designer. However, if we always waited until we were experts in a field before we tried it, would we ever do anything? In my earliest days as a web designer, I had the same feeling as I'd had way back when we brought home that box of pipes and connectors, "I can now build whatever I want." It may have taken thirty plugins, but I felt like I could build anything. Unfortunately, that feeling didn't last. My sites crashed as soon as the first plugin updated. Those first websites were like pieces of art held together by duct tape, but they were my creations, and with every crashed site I learned a little bit more about "what not to do."

Fast forward another couple of years. I was working on a hackathon project with accomplished developers, database engineers, and graphic designers. I had that old feeling again, "We can now build whatever we want." Guess what? We did! The app that we built went on to win a state award. From that project to now, I have never lost "the feeling." Even though teams and projects—and products and companies—have changed through the years, I still believe I can build anything.

Why does this matter? Why do I care about this feeling? I care because companies are terrific at squashing childlike feelings, and stamping them out of their employees. They don't do it on purpose; it just happens. As product managers, we MUST keep that attitude alive. We must start with the mindset that anything is possible, and then filter down to whether the idea is wise depending on time and resources.

I take this attitude with me when I attend planning meetings for future products. Here is an example of how this looks: let's say that I am a product manager for Yelp or any similar food review/recommendation service. I would start a meeting about future product features and development by imagining what the most impressive food experience would look like. What is the best experience I can imagine as someone looking for lunch or dinner?

I might suggest, "What if an app started to learn your eating behaviors based on time of week, season, or temperature?

Then it learned what dishes you ordered during those times. It learned how much you typically spend during different times of the week and your preferred wait time. It could also learn how far you typically like to go from your location to find food. It then would not only suggest a restaurant but a dish from there. It would learn what dishes people with similar tastes enjoy. Eventually, it could get smart enough to automatically order that dish for you and deliver it at your preferred eating time."

EVERY SINGLE ONE OF YOU reading this book immediately started thinking of reasons why the features I described would not work.

STOP IT.

You must first have the attitude that anything is possible. Don't limit the creativity within you and your team. Let yourselves dream up kick-ass products whether they are feasible or not. Your future product won't be amazing if you are not the one who encourages everyone to dream. If you don't have that "what if…" attitude, you will view your product within its current constraints. At best, this will lead to only marginal feature improvements, quarter after quarter. That's not good enough.

By the way, if you decide to develop what I described above, write me in as a one-percent owner. Then we can both sit overlooking the beach while my Pho is automatically delivered at 5:45 pm on Tuesday, September 10th.

Take a moment to dream. What would the most amazing version of your product be? Fill in the dream bubble below:

Fantastic! Next, break the big ideas into ideas that make sense based on time and resources.

Let's take a look back at the example I gave, "…an app that learns how much you typically spend during different times of the week and your preferred wait time." You want to have a feature similar to this developed. First of all, you realize that the food app can't learn how much a person is spending because their purchase is made either over the phone, or with cash or credit card during pickup. However, it can learn at what times a user consistently uses the app. It can learn what the last restaurant they looked at was. It can know what interactions they made with that page. Therefore the feature may not be able to include the price spent, but it could collect data on the other elements. If you hadn't allowed yourself to dream, you wouldn't have even explored this possibility. When you don't explore possibilities, you end up building the same things as everyone else.

Action Item. Schedule a meeting for a month from now. Make it a two-hour session in a room full of whiteboards. Invite team members who are good at brainstorming. Start the meeting by asking the question from the dream bubble, "What would the most amazing version of our product be?" Capture all the ideas and thoughts people have. The goal is quantity not quality.
At the end of the meeting, write down all the ideas or take pictures of the whiteboards. This session should provide enough work to keep the engineering team busy for months.

Offense or Defense

"Defense wins championships."
"The best defense is a good offense."

You may have heard of these sayings or similar ones. As you know from this book, I have a love for both playing and watching sports. However, this isn't another sports analogy.

I read an article once that asked a product manager how they operated. Were they defensive- or offensive-minded? Here is a quick way to tell which one you are: "If your main competitor introduced a fantastic new feature, would you, A) figure out a way to make a similar feature, or B) come up with a completely unique, new feature for your own product? If you choose option A you are defensive-minded. If you chose option B you are offensive-minded. There are pros and cons to each mindset. I am almost completely offensive-minded. I don't care what the competition is doing; I just want to build new and exciting features that push the envelope. I've hired product managers who are defensive-minded. They have typically cared about whether or not our product matches the industry, and if it compares "apples to apples" with other products.

If you are a defensively minded product manager, you are more inclined to focus on:
- Churn
- LTV
- Customer Reviews
- Conventional Designs
- Technical Debt

If you are an offensively minded product manager, you are more inclined to focus on:
- Emerging Technologies

- Growth Percentage
- Early Adopters
- Speed

On the graph below, which has defense on the left and offense on the right, mark where you naturally think and operate.

Defense   Offense

Your company is in the strongest position when it has a mix of product managers who have different mindsets. As an offensive-minded product manager, I need to learn to care more about the defense aspects of our product. Even though I bring great value by thinking offensively, there will be weaknesses in the product if I don't force myself to think about defense.

If you are defensive-minded, here are some things to focus on:

- Watch for and read about new technology releases. Learn about what is becoming possible.
- Spend more time in the dream bubble that we previously discussed.

- Keep your product's growth percent always in front of you.
- Explore other marketing verticals.

If you are offensive-minded, here are some things for you to focus on:
- What small companies are starting to gain traction?
- What areas in your tech stack are not sustainable?
- When you did the competitor analysis earlier in this book, which features from your competitor's products might be worth building?
- How many bugs are being reported in each release?

Has your product historically been more offensive- or defensive-focused?

Is your leadership team offensive- or defensive-focused?

CHAPTER 15

BRINGING IT ALL TOGETHER

We have covered so much in this book, and yet we have covered so little. Any one of these chapters probably sent you down several long rabbit holes, and they all left you with more to learn. The joy of being a product manager is never running out of things to learn or ideas to pursue. Here is the bad news, ninety percent of the learning process is worthless. We learn something, get excited about it, our phone buzzes or some other distraction comes up, and we forget it. Do you remember the last conference you went to? There were probably some excellent sessions, right? Make a list of one thing you learned in each session and then write out three things that you actually took action on since that conference

.

.
.
.

I didn't give you a box to do that in because it was an impossible task. Most humans are terrible at retaining knowledge, especially when large amounts are consumed in short periods of time.

I hate wasting my time. I hate it even more when other people waste my time. My goal when writing this book was not to waste anyone's time. I consider it wasted time if I read something good and then forget it two weeks later. Once I made a goal to read one book a month for a year. In October of that year, a friend asked me what I had learned from the book I read in January. I couldn't tell them one thing. I gave some broad details but I had remembered and applied absolutely nothing from that book to my life. Sorry Charles Duhigg! From that experience, I realized that the most valuable information to be found is that which you go and find for yourself. This is also the information you will remember and actually use.

I don't want you to "do" product management the way I do product management. Your circumstances are entirely different from mine. However, I do want you to know and remember the information that matters in your company. The knowledge you have learned about your specific product, by following these exercises, needs to override a concept you read last week in some random article. That feature or idea may work well for business "X," but it won't translate 1:1 to yours. You might even need to override some of the practices that you used in your last job.

I hope that at least a handful of the activities provided in this book have been useful for you. Now it's time to bring it all together. Below are what I call "Product-Feature Cards." They are used to determine the viability and priority of product features quickly. By filling out these cards, you can drastically reduce the chances of developing features that are not aligned to your business or your customers.

Every organization has different tools and systems they use as roadmaps and for coordinating work with the engineer/developer team. These product cards are not meant to replace or override your existing systems, but rather, they are simply a quick way to have a holistic view of various features.

PRODUCT FEATURE

Feature Name: _____

- Describe the functionality as if you were describing it to your grandma:

- Customer group most impacted:
  (Customer Profile)

- Stakeholder most impacted:
  (Stakeholder Profile)

- What does success look like? How will it be measured?

Product Differentiation (Circle One)

Low (3) (2) (1) High

Value Added to the Customer

Low (3) (2) (1) High

Resources Required

Low (1) (2) (3) High

Development Time

Low (1) (2) (3) High

Total: _____

PRODUCT FEATURE

Feature Name: _____

- Describe the functionality as if you were describing it to your grandma:

- Customer group most impacted:
  (Customer Profile)

- Stakeholder most impacted:
  (Stakeholder Profile)

- What does success look like? How will it be measured?

Product Differentiation (Circle One)

Low (3) (2) (1) High

Value Added to the Customer

Low (3) (2) (1) High

Resources Required

Low (1) (2) (3) High

Development Time

Low (1) (2) (3) High

Total: _____

PRODUCT FEATURE

Feature Name: _____

- Describe the functionality as if you were describing it to your grandma:

- Customer group most impacted:
  (Customer Profile)

- Stakeholder most impacted:
  (Stakeholder Profile)

- What does success look like? How will it be measured?

Product Differentiation (Circle One)

Low   (3)   (2)   (1)   High

Value Added to the Customer

Low   (3)   (2)   (1)   High

Resources Required

Low   (1)   (2)   (3)   High

Development Time

Low   (1)   (2)   (3)   High

Total: _____

PRODUCT FEATURE

Feature Name: _____

- Describe the functionality as if you were describing it to your grandma:

- Customer group most impacted:
  (Customer Profile)

- Stakeholder most impacted:
  (Stakeholder Profile)

- What does success look like? How will it be measured?

Product Differentiation (Circle One)

Low (3) (2) (1) High

Value Added to the Customer

Low (3) (2) (1) High

Resources Required

Low (1) (2) (3) High

Development Time

Low (1) (2) (3) High

Total: _____

PRODUCT FEATURE

Feature Name: _____

- Describe the functionality as if you were describing it to your grandma:

- Customer group most impacted:
  (Customer Profile)

- Stakeholder most impacted:
  (Stakeholder Profile)

- What does success look like? How will it be measured?

Product Differentiation (Circle One)

Low ③ ② ① High

Value Added to the Customer

Low ③ ② ① High

Resources Required

Low ① ② ③ High

Development Time

Low ① ② ③ High

Total: _____

At the bottom of the card, add up the numbers from the lower section. If you filled out several cards, sort them from lowest to highest. The card with the lowest number will be the "quick win." The card with the highest number will be what I have heard referred to as a "thankless task." If you have never built a roadmap or struggle to know how to prioritize items, this exercise will make it easy for you to get started.

Remember the movie *Up?* The one that makes everyone cry in the first five minutes when the old man's wife dies, and then his house is lifted up and away by helium balloons? It is a great movie, and I should watch it again. In the movie there is a dog named Dug. He is most famous for suddenly saying "Squirrel!" and getting distracted from everything else that is happening.[12] At my company, we actually have things called "squirrel goals." They are items that come up during the day and distract us from what we are supposed to be doing.

I would argue that there are "squirrel" product features. These would be the features that randomly appear and suddenly become the most important thing to build. They attract everyone's attention because they appear to be a golden ticket to exponential product growth. Remember last quarter's well-thought-out plan for product releases? That is tossed to the side to make room for this new feature.

Squirrel product features appear to be fun, exciting, and groundbreaking. However, ninety-nine percent of the time, they turn out to be the opposite.

I hope these cards will help you avoid squirrel product features. I think you'll find that they will also help you to be prepared for any meeting. When a C-Level person walks in and says, "Why are we building this?" you will be able to say, "We are building 'X' feature to solve 'Y' problem for this group of (customers/stakeholders). I hypothesize that it will impact 'Z' number, and we will measure it this way. We are doing this feature next because the expected return is higher than the resources it will take." Not only will this make you look good as a product manager, it will also protect the product from getting sabotaged by squirrel goals from either inside or outside your team.

As a rule of thumb, before adding a feature on the roadmap, first fill out a product-feature card. No one else has to see these cards. Taking the ten minutes to fill a card out for each feature will ensure that you are well prepared in every meeting.

CONCLUSION

You can read yourself to death with different philosophies pertaining to roadmaps, product backlogs, user stories, company organization, and everything else under the sun. While there is a time and place to figure out how to use any of those philosophies with your team, they won't matter if your product doesn't have a strong foundation. Remember, what you do in your first ninety days as a product manager will impact the rest of your time with the company. Your early decisions will form coworker opinions and set the tone for your work environment. I hope this book and these exercises will help you lay a strong foundation that will build trust and respect for you and your team. I hope you filled out the exercises and that you will reference them in the future.

The final task is to add three events to your calendar. One for six months from now, one for one year from now, and one for two years from now. Block out two hours for yourself to read back through all the exercises and questions you answered in the book. Some of the answers will no longer be true and will serve as launch points to find the new information you need. Other answers will remind you of key information you may have forgotten.

You can and will be a great product manager. I am excited about all of the amazing features and products you will build!

For additional resources or to get in touch with John, visit First90.co

ACKNOWLEDGEMENTS

I believe everyone you meet influences your life in some small way. They shift the way you think or offer a new perspective. Then there are certain people in your life that are responsible for not just influencing but actually changing the course of your life. I wouldn't be who I am without them and this book wouldn't exist. I specifically think of the impact that my wife, my dad, Bret, and Caleb have had on me. You are my inspirations.

I also want to thank my editor Shawn for tirelessly going through the book multiple times and making my writing clear and focused.

Finally, a thank you to all the product managers who have influenced me with their writing, videos, and books. By being generous with your content, I was able to navigate my first 90 days as a product manager.

NOTES

1 "Product Manager job description," Workable, accessed September 28, 2020, https://resources.workable.com/product-manager-job-description.

2 Dale Carnegie, How To Win Friends And Influence People (New York: Pocket Books, 1936).

3 "Groupthink," Psychology Today, accessed September 28, 2020, https://www.psychologytoday.com/us/basics/groupthink.

4 National Automobile Chamber of Commerce, Inc., "Motor Vehicle Registrations, 1895-1929," in Facts and Figures of the Automobile Industry (New York: National Automobile Chamber of Commerce, 1920), 15, https://www.railsandtrails.com/AutoFacts/.

5 Malcolm Gladwell, The Tipping Point: How Little Things Can Make a Big Difference (New York: Little, Brown and Company, 2000).

6 Kathy Sierra, Badass: Making Users Awesome (Sebastopol: O'Reilly Media Inc, 2015).

7 Chris McChesney and Sean Covey, 4 Disciplines of Execution: Achieving Your Wildly Important Goals (New York: Free Press, 2012).

8 "Site Explorer," Ahrefs, accessed September 30, 2020, https://ahrefs.com/positions-explorer/organic-keywords/v5/subdomains/us/all/all/all/all/all/all/all/1/traffic_desc?target=monday.com.

9 "Site Explorer," Ahrefs, accessed September 30, 2020, https://ahrefs.com/positions-explorer/organic-keywords/v5/subdomains/us/all/all/all/all/all/all/all/1/traffic_desc?target=airtable.com.

10 The Office, Season 5, episode 7, "Customer Survey," directed by Stephen Merchant, written by Lester Lewis, featuring John Krasinski, Rainn Wilson, Jenna Fischer, Ed Helms, and Angela Kinsey, aired November 6, 2008, in broadcast syndication. https://www.netflix.com/title/70136120.

11 "Season 5 - Episode 06 'Customer Survey'," Officequotes.net, 2017, https://www.officequotes.net/no5-06.php.

12 Up, directed by Pete Docter (Burbank, CA: Walt Disney Pictures and Pixar Animation Studios, 2009), DVD.

Made in United States
Orlando, FL
08 March 2022